The Return to Study Handbook

The Return to Study Handbook

Study skills for mature, distance and workplace learners

Chloe Burroughs

> **Publisher's note**
> Every possible effort has been made to ensure that the information contained in this book is accurate at the time of going to press, and the publishers and authors cannot accept responsibility for any errors or omissions, however caused. No responsibility for loss or damage occasioned to any person acting, or refraining from action, as a result of the material in this publication can be accepted by the editor, the publisher or the author.

First published in Great Britain and the United States in 2019 by Kogan Page Limited

Apart from any fair dealing for the purposes of research or private study, or criticism or review, as permitted under the Copyright, Designs and Patents Act 1988, this publication may only be reproduced, stored or transmitted, in any form or by any means, with the prior permission in writing of the publishers, or in the case of reprographic reproduction in accordance with the terms and licences issued by the CLA. Enquiries concerning reproduction outside these terms should be sent to the publishers at the undermentioned addresses:

2nd Floor, 45 Gee Street	122 W 27th St, 10th Floor	4737/23 Ansari Road
London	New York, NY 10001	Daryaganj
EC1V 3RS	USA	New Delhi 110002
United Kingdom		India

www.koganpage.com

© Chloe Burroughs, 2019

The right of Chloe Burroughs to be identified as the author of this work has been asserted by her in accordance with the Copyright, Designs and Patents Act 1988.

ISBNs

Hardback	978 1 78966 024 1
Paperback	978 0 7494 9690 6
Ebook	978 0 7494 9691 3

British Library Cataloguing-in-Publication Data

A CIP record for this book is available from the British Library.

Library of Congress Cataloging-in-Publication Data

Names: Burroughs, Chloe, author.
Title: The return to study handbook : study skills for mature, distance, and workplace learners / Chloe Burroughs.
Description: London ; New York : Kogan Page Limited, 2019. | Includes index.
Identifiers: LCCN 2019014094 (print) | LCCN 2019981105 (ebook) | ISBN 9781789660241 (hardback) | ISBN 9780749496906 (paperback) | ISBN 9780749496913 (ebook)
Subjects: LCSH: Study skills. | Adult education.
Classification: LCC LC5225.M47 B87 2019 (print) | LCC LC5225.M47 (ebook) | DDC 371.30281–dc23
LC record available at https://lccn.loc.gov/2019014094
LC ebook record available at https://lccn.loc.gov/2019981105

Typeset by Integra Software Services, Pondicherry
Print production managed by Jellyfish
Printed and bound by CPI Group (UK) Ltd, Croydon CR0 4YY

Mum, I love you.
Thank you for being 'that' proud mother,
for believing in me always, and for giving
me everything worth having.

CONTENTS

About the author xi
Foreword by Dr Liz Marr xiii
Acknowledgements xv

Introduction 1

PART ONE Getting ready for further study 5

01 **Independent learning** 7
Sink or swim 7
Independent learning skills 9

02 **Embrace your non-traditionalism as a student** 13
Mature students 14
Distance learners 17
Workplace learners 21

03 **How to prepare for higher education** 27
How to prepare for your first (or next) module 27
How to start each module with a bang 32
Advice for new students 34
The importance of your support network 36

04 **Goal setting** 39
Why set study goals? 39
What study goals should I set myself? 40
Seven steps for setting epic study goals 41
Make it happen 45

PART TWO Mindset and motivation 49

05 Mindset 51
Talent vs hard work 52
Fixed vs growth mindset 54
Mindset gremlins 58
The power of positivity 63

06 Motivation 67
One-day motivation 67
Everyday motivation 68
The big motivation myth 69
What to do when you don't feel like studying 74

PART THREE Organization and productivity 77

07 Organization 79
Physical studying organization 79
Digital studying organization 80
The importance of backups 82
How to prepare yourself and your space 84
How to create an awesome study plan 88
How to actually stick to your study plan 90
Work–life balance 92

08 Productivity 95
Best study self 95
How to plan for a productive week 97
Study session planner 99
Study breaks 101
The Pomodoro Technique 102
The dangers of multitasking 104
How to study effectively when you have a job 105
How to study with a family 108
How to create a kick-butt study routine 111

09   **The dark side of productivity** 113
     The five-step anti-procrastination method 114
     How to deal with overwhelm 121
     How to study when you're tired 123
     How to catch up when you've fallen behind 125
     Self-care over burnout 127

PART FOUR   Classes, note taking and assignment skills 131

10   **Classes** 133
     The importance of attending classes 134
     How to get the most out of your classes 135
     Class troubleshooting 138

11   **Note taking** 140
     Common note-taking mistakes 140
     Taking great notes 142
     Note-taking location clues 144
     Note-taking content clues 145
     How to take notes 146

12   **Essay writing** 155
     Planning 155
     Writing 160
     Editing 168

PART FIVE   Exam preparation 173

13   **Exam revision** 175
     Exam investigation 175
     Key exam principles 179
     Active revision techniques 182
     Specific techniques for different exam types 187
     Advice for multiple exams 189
     The three core revision activities 190
     Create a revision plan 192
     How to develop a positive revision mindset 193

14 Exam performance 195
How to develop a positive exam mindset 195
How to prepare for your upcoming exam 197
How to kick butt in your exam 198
What to do after your exam 201

PART SIX Personal development 203

15 Continuous improvement 205
Three ways you can shake up your studying to achieve the grades you really want 206
You are a good student 210

References 213
Index 217

ABOUT THE AUTHOR

Chloe Burroughs is a study skills expert who teaches non-traditional students how to study effectively. She left school at 18 with low grades and even lower self-confidence… so she ran away to Barbados instead of going to university like the rest of her friends.

A few years later, when she was back in the UK, Chloe plucked up the courage to enrol in university and study alongside her full-time job. After four years of hard work, weekends stuck inside, and *a lot* of chocolate, she achieved a first-class business degree.

Realizing she must be pretty good at this studying malarkey, Chloe set up her own business as a study skills trainer which she now runs full-time with the help of more hard work and chocolate. She believes that with perseverance, a strong mindset, and smart study strategies, anyone can achieve academic success.

Chloe provides coaching and online courses to help students master the study techniques they need to become productive, confident learners. Visit chloeburroughs.com to read one of her strategy-packed blog posts, listen to an episode of her study skills podcast, or enrol in one of her courses.

When she's not helping students uplevel their study skills, you can find Chloe eating Thai food, getting lost on walks, or hosting loud, solo concerts in her car. Chloe has yet to find anyone who can beat her at Harry Potter trivia…

FOREWORD

When I was asked if I might consider writing a foreword for this book, my immediate response was yes, of course. Why would I not want to endorse such a useful text by a graduate of the institution for which I am so proud to work? But, this was yet another thing I had added to my quite substantial to-do list! So, it was a real pleasure when I read the text to be reminded of all the useful techniques I could adopt to complete this and all my other tasks.

Chloe has produced an invaluable and completely down-to-earth resource for anyone who has committed to taking on something new in their life. Any new goal presents fresh challenges and obstacles which, although scary and possibly overwhelming, are just part of the journey. Returning to study, preparing to run a marathon, starting a family, preparing for a new career; these are wildly different yet all require learning new skills, knowledge, motivation, resilience and commitment.

For an individual returning to study as a mature, distance or workplace learner, setting out on the journey can be terrifying, especially when they have been out of education for many years. Very often, the root of that fear lies in perceived earlier failures, making it even more difficult for them to subject themselves to the risk of a repeat. But the other elephants in the room include the time we think we have before we start and the time we actually have once we get underway. Then there are the occasions when we feel too exhausted, not in the mood for study or just simply unmotivated. If and when we manage to get over all of these mountains, we find we have then to learn a whole new set of skills to help us study effectively.

Having been a mature student myself, with a very young child, a poor school performance behind me and the necessity to earn while I learned, the contents of this book resonated strongly with me. When you have felt put down in the past by exam failures it is very hard to restore your self-belief, resilience and motivation. Just as for Chloe, it was the Open University which did this for me too, through its focus on support for learning and the quality of its teaching material. But more than this, it gave me study skills and techniques which I had never before experienced. Having bought into the idea at school that I just wasn't clever enough, I suddenly discovered that there were all kinds of techniques to help me to succeed and which I have been able to carry forward into all my subsequent learning journeys.

Through the early part of her book, Chloe provides a whole host of top tips which actually might also be great life hacks. Positive self-talk, organizing your workspace and your study timetable, rewarding completion of goals, negotiating support for childcare or housework – all really practical ways of ensuring you can meet your deadlines and be successful. Personally, I used to find it particularly helpful to visualize my success (and still do!) – imagining myself walking across the platform to collect my degree in front of my family and friends.

As Chloe suggests, give this book a thorough read in the first instance, then dip back into parts as needed. But as she also says, you do need to take action. Chloe writes in an engaging and encouraging way and her 'action steps' are pragmatic but more importantly very doable. Having refreshed my own organizational thinking with this book, I reviewed and re-prioritized my to-do list according to the task's size and deadline, went for a few quick wins and happily finished this foreword with two days to spare! Thanks, Chloe. Now for my reward.

Dr Liz Marr
Pro Vice Chancellor (Students)
The Open University

ACKNOWLEDGEMENTS

Aged seven I decided I was going to become a famous author. I was a voracious reader and wanted nothing more than to attend one of Enid Blyton's fictional boarding schools or J K Rowling's Hogwarts.

The dream was replaced with many others over the years until I forgot it ever existed. That was until Rebecca Bush, my editor at Kogan Page, contacted me about writing this book. It wouldn't have happened without you so thank you for turning that faded ember of a dream into a flame to be kindled. Your confidence in me, even when I started doubting myself, really helped me through this process – and to even enjoy it!

Unfortunately, the world doesn't stop when you write a book. Locking myself away and writing thousands of words per day would not have been possible without my boyfriend Dominic. Nor would the years before that where I completed my degree and launched my business on top of my fulltime job. Thank you for keeping me fed and putting up with the little spare time I had without ever making me feel guilty. I've never needed loud cheerleading from you because your quiet, unquestionable confidence in me gives me confidence in myself.

I want to thank my beautiful mummy, Sandra, and sisters, Lucy and Stephanie, for always knowing what I need; whether that's distraction, a pep talk, or a kick up the butt. I also want to thank Lucy (and I suppose her husband Chris too) for giving me the gift of my wonderful nephew William. Taking breaks to belly laugh together and teach him how to say 'boobies' (not at all sorry) definitely helped me push through.

I have the most incredible bunch of best friends from school that truly light up my life and motivate me to work hard. Lucy French, Hattie Jordan, Lily Byham, Nour Sidawi, Emily Mummery, Helen Bell, Becky Higgs, Alice Dale, Louise Fenner, Yvonne Beach, Sarah Mann and Martha Dorey. Thank you for all your support and confidence in me, along with our shared need to always eat three meals a day plus snacks, and your uncanny ability to remember every dodgy date and drunken escapade.

Extra special thanks are needed for a few of you. Lily, thank you for being the best housemate, loyal friend and yoga-retreat adventurer.

Nour, where the hell do I start?! You started off as the weird girl who sat next to me on the bus on the first day of school and now you're the dependable constant in my life that I need for shared tea snobbery, Harry Potter chats and world domination planning. Thank you.

To Hattie and Lucy, my co-members of the DA (yep, that's right, Dumbledore's Army). Thank you for your unwavering, relentless support of me throughout my studies, business building and book writing. I deeply appreciate our friendship that encompasses inane, rambling voice notes, secret sharing, and conversations on feminism, food and our favourite murders.

This book would not have been written without the help of my Pomodoro Pals, Emma Perols, Kay Fabella, Janneke Den Draak and Alessia Pandolfi. The last few months of book writing coincided with me quitting my job and you guys gave me the routine I so needed. Thank you for being my virtual work buddies in five different countries.

Special thanks go to Emma Perols, a fast friend I didn't know I needed and now I couldn't be without, and Kay Fabella, who helped me believe that I can tell a good story.

Writing a book and running a business takes courage and determination, and the ability to ask for help. I want to thank Fran Excell for always knowing when I'm hiding, using your mind magic to get me out of my own head, and for keeping me going with silliness and love.

Finally, to all those who've been necessary and wonderful companions on my journey so far: Jim Thompson, Jeni Worthy, Dan Worthy, Heather Gray, Jessica Lorimer and the rest of the Dotties.

Introduction

It's Monday morning and I'm sat in the corner meeting room of our office, exactly a week after I joined the company as an administrator. The 10 of us assemble and my manager starts the team meeting. I scribble down actions for the next hour, eager to impress, until, in the last few minutes, my manager turns to me.

'Chloe, HR have asked for an update of our personnel files', he says. 'Can you go through and check they're up to date? They also want copies of all of our qualification certificates.'

I note down the action but immediately my brow furrows as I try and remember where mine are. After the meeting I catch my manager in his office and say nervously, 'Erm, about that last action… I don't actually know where my certificates from sixth form are. How much of a problem will that be?'

My manager grabs his laptop and empty mug and then looks at me. 'What? Oh, Chloe, A-levels don't matter. The only qualifications that count are from university, so don't worry.'

And with that, my manager heads out of the office for his next meeting, leaving me feeling like I've been kicked in the chest.

Looking back, I know that my manager wasn't trying to be dismissive, but I immediately felt ashamed. I was hit with so many bad memories from my last years in formal education.

I loved learning as a child and was able to get good grades without trying too hard, but everything changed during my time at sixth form. The workload was a massive step up and I didn't seem to get the memo that hard work was needed. I thought I could just 'wing it'… but boy was I wrong.

Within the first few months, I failed my first physics exam and was told I'd have to work harder… so I dropped the subject. Maths was also a problem. I arrived late to class, didn't do the homework and never brought the right equipment. I failed so many exams that my school tried to kick me out of the class. Now, I'm ashamed of how I acted but back then I was angry and expected my tutors to help me even though I wasn't helping myself.

This culminated in me leaving school with low grades and even lower self-esteem. My confidence was shattered, and I decided not to go to university because I believed I wasn't intelligent enough.

Over the next four years I lived and worked in Barbados, then came home and worked in an entry-level job. Through travelling and working, my confidence and ambition grew and I no longer ran away from hard work. Which is why that conversation with my manager was such a knock – that negative time in my life had caught up with me. I felt like I wasn't part of the conversation, and that I never would be because I didn't go to university. I knew that I didn't *need* to return to study, because my self-worth shouldn't be defined by a qualification, but in that moment I realized *I wanted it*. That conversation lit a fire inside me that I thought had long since been smothered. I was ready to give studying another go.

Fast-forward a few months and I've squeezed a desk into my bedroom at my mum's house and am trying to fit my business degree around a full-time job and a two-hour daily commute. However, it became clear *pretty* quickly that I didn't know what I was doing.

At university or college, our tutors' time and resources are allotted to deliver the material we need to pass, not to teach us the strategies we need to do well. They teach us *what* to learn, but they don't teach us *how* to learn.

I didn't know how to organize my time, take notes, stay motivated, write essays or pass exams. All I did know was that I wasn't willing to invest a lot of my time, energy and money over the next few years and not come out of it with a grade I was proud of.

So, alongside all my studying I started researching *how* to study effectively. I experimented with different methods and created some of my own until my study skills and grades were improving with every essay and exam.

After four long years I did it. I walked across that stage and graduated with a first-class degree and a first-class grin on my face. Eighteen-year-old Chloe would have laughed if I'd told her what was to come, and she'd have fallen on the floor if I'd told her I'd now be working full time, running a business helping other students walk this same journey.

Completing my degree taught me two valuable lessons. Firstly, there isn't one opportunity to go to university or college. If you blink aged 18 you won't miss it. When you're ready to return to study, your education will be there waiting for you.

And secondly, academic success isn't just about natural talent (because if it was, I wouldn't be here writing this book!). All of us, with the right mindset, work ethic and study strategies, can achieve grades we can be proud of.

For a lot of students, me included, there's a big gap between working our butts off and wanting academic success… and actually achieving it. That gap is study skills – and this book will help you plug the hole. I'm going to share with you my tried-and-tested strategies for effective studying, so you can improve your confidence as a learner and develop your study skills to help you achieve your goals – whether it's that dream job, promotion, career change… or simply framing the qualification certificate you've always wanted.

How to use this book

This book is structured like a roadmap. We'll start with the introductory work around preparing for higher education and setting study goals. Next, we'll cover the foundational study skills: developing a strong mindset, staying motivated, organizing yourself and your time, and being super productive. Then, it's onto the core study skills of doing well in your classes and learning how to take effective notes that serve you in your essays and exams. Next, we'll dive into assessment skills – the specific strategies you need to do well in your essays and exams. And, finally, we'll talk about how to improve your study skills so that your grades keep increasing.

I recommend reading the book in order first, as each chapter will build on the last – but then I recommend you treat it like your personal studying handbook. Whenever you come across a challenge, return to the relevant chapter to find a solution.

My best tip, though, is don't just *read* this book. Take action! It's easy to read a book, nod your head and then put it to one side, but action is what it will take to achieve those higher grades. That's why, in this book, each chapter ends with a summary of the key action steps you should take to reap the benefits in your own studies.

I'm going to leave you with a reminder as you explore the rest of this book. By deciding to return to study, you have taken a *massive* step in the direction of the future you want. It's normal to feel some doubts, and there will be challenging and confusing times in your studying journey. But you *can* do this. Trust in the wisdom that made you decide to return to study, and lean on the resources you have at your disposal – your motivation, your determination, and this book. Now go kick some studying butt!

Part One
Getting ready for further study

01
Independent learning

Studying at university or college, or in a professional context, requires a different set of skills than studying at school. At school, your teachers are largely responsible for your learning. They will remind you of upcoming due dates and may even be lenient if you miss them; if they see you're struggling, they will step in and try to help you. They will speak up if they think you're not reaching your full potential. Most of my school reports conveyed the same message: 'Chloe has great potential, she just needs to stop chatting and work a bit harder.'

After compulsory education, however, this accountability shifts almost completely to the student – you become responsible for your own learning and education. Your tutors will be assigned a greater number of students and your face time with them decreases – for distance learners, you may have no face time with your tutors at all. Some courses may have 10 or more hours a week of teaching, whereas others may not even have one hour a week. If you don't put the effort in, your tutor is not going to encourage you to work harder for your own success and future. If you want help at university or college you have to ask for it.

Sink or swim

The shift in responsibility itself is not really the problem. The problem is that it's not talked about. Your first day of higher education doesn't include a sit down where you're told that you're now responsible for your own learning. No other kind of learning is handled this way, really – picture yourself learning to swim as a child. You start your swimming journey with a parent near you and you wear armbands to keep you afloat and safe. You're told that the aim is to swim independently, and you work up to this goal slowly. The air is gradually let out of the armbands and soon you feel ready to try swimming without them. But in higher education, becoming an independent learner is not this gradual, supported process. The armbands are taken off without warning and without you being taught how to swim first.

Some get over the shock quickly, or take to the new environment immediately; after a few test strokes, they find a rhythm and are off. But not everyone finds it so easy. Maybe you start panicking. You go under and pop back up in a flail of limbs. Water is splashing in your face and you feel alone. You look up and see someone walking along the edge of the pool and you shout to them, 'Help! I don't know how to swim!'. They reply, with a look of confusion on their face, 'Why not? Swimming is easy. Other people know how to swim.'

Some students adapt to higher education more easily than others. They don't need to be told about the responsibility shift, and they develop independent learning skills almost subconsciously. However, for other students, like learning to swim without armbands, adjusting to the demands of university or college is more difficult. I was a flailing, panicking would-be swimmer *and* student. It took me until I was 20 to learn how to swim, and it took me until the end of my first year of university before I started feeling more confident and had developed independent learning skills.

For those students who don't adjust well to the shift, higher education is harder than it needs to be. Maybe you enrolled in your course, nervous because you didn't do great at school. You really want to achieve a degree… but your excitement is laced with doubts. You start studying but feel unsteady; you're not sure *how* you should be studying. Your motivation drops off as you quickly become overwhelmed. Your doubts are becoming realized and you worry that you're not good enough, that you're just an imposter and that everyone is ahead of you.

If this is you: don't panic! Those feelings are almost certainly not true. What *is* true, though, is that this vital transition isn't talked about, and we are not given any guidance and support to walk through it. Unlike swimming lessons, we don't have the luxury of time to learn to become an effective, independent student; every day, week, month we spend using ineffective strategies costs us energy, money and grades.

The solution is two-fold. Firstly, you must become responsible for your own learning and success and secondly, you need to learn *how* to develop the skills to become an independent learner.

> **Study skills can be learned**
>
> A client came to me earlier this year because his essay grades were low. Through working with him, I discovered he struggled to get his thoughts down on paper, to turn his ideas into coherent arguments. It wasn't that he lacked the knowledge, talent, or understanding; he could talk to me for hours about his subject and the theories he'd been learning, but this wasn't translating into good essay scores. After teaching him *how* to write essays, his potential unlocked and his essay grades have climbed since. Just like him, if you know the best way to approach each study problem, you will be able to achieve the grades your hard work deserves.

Independent learning skills

If you want to achieve high grades, as we've seen, you need to take responsibility for your own study skills and learning. This means being an independent learner: a student who takes responsibility for their own education. Becoming an independent learner will help you deal with the shift in responsibility in higher education and master the study skills you need to flourish.

In my experience, there are five essential skills of every successful independent learner. In later chapters we'll dive into each study skill in more depth and look at the key strategies you need to know, but for now, here's a quick overview.

1 *Motivation and self-belief*

Every student (me included) has days where they don't want to study. It's easy to sit on on the sofa and put off studying until you 'feel like it'. But that inspiration may never come! An independent learner must discover how to motivate themselves, so they can study even when they don't really want to. You don't have to be Hermione Granger-style motivated all the time, because you can do great work even when you're *un*motivated. In Chapter 6 we'll look at lots of ways of boosting your motivation so you can get the job done.

An independent learner must develop confidence and belief in themselves, their abilities and their power to change. Remember: our *past* grades don't dictate our *future* grades – and our past mistakes don't have to be repeated. Over time, it's possible to develop a growth mindset: the belief that your intelligence is malleable and can be increased through effort and the right study strategies. We'll look more at this in Chapter 5.

2 Organization and time management

Organization is a bit of a dirty word for some people, an unobtainable goal. But don't worry – I'm not asking you to become super-efficient overnight! Instead, try these three things to become an independent learner, and reduce panic and overwhelm in your studies.

- **Your due dates should never surprise you.** Don't rely on your memory or other students reminding you of deadlines, as this is a sure-fire way to achieve lower grades than you want. Instead, record all important tutorial, project and assignment dates in a way you will use.

- **Independent learners plan their study time holistically,** taking into account their other commitments. Spend some time each week looking at both your workload and your schedule. Work backwards from any due dates, to make sure you fit in enough study sessions to submit work that makes you proud.

- **Organize your physical and digital to save time, energy and your sanity.** Spend an hour setting up a simple, digital folder structure and creating a physical system of folders and notebooks for your handwritten and printed materials (more on this in Chapter 7).

3 Problem solving and initiative

Throughout your studies there are going to be approximately 2,852 instances where you get stuck and don't know how to unstick yourself to move on. Maybe you'll come across a tricky concept you can't grasp, or perhaps your essay question will fly over your head and you won't know where to start. Taking initiative is an important skill for independent learners, and it's even more vital if you're also a distance learner, when getting help from a tutor is not as simple as raising a hand in class or walking to their office to have a chat.

During a recent study skills training, I asked the attendees to share what they do when they meet a problem in their studies. Here are their suggestions, to give you some ideas:

- take a break and go for a short walk;
- search on Google for resources that could help;
- sleep on it and try again tomorrow;
- search YouTube for tutorial videos;
- try to explain the concept in simple terms to someone who doesn't study your subject;
- discuss your problem with a fellow student;
- contact your tutor and ask for help.

If you try to solve the problem yourself and can't, it's time to ask for help. Don't waste time sitting in confusion; reach out to your tutors and see what can be done. Some people don't like asking for help because, yes, there's a chance your tutor will tell you they can't answer a specific question. But there's also a chance they can give you the exact piece of advice you need to get unstuck and move forward.

4 Self-development focus

You cannot grow and improve unless you're willing to change. If you want higher grades, or you want to achieve the same grades in less time and with less stress, then you need to test out new study techniques to change your skills and habits. An independent learner is willing to switch up how they study, and understands that different modules and subjects are better suited to some study methods over others.

As well as changing up how you study, a simple way of improving your grades is to seek out – and *act on* – all tutor feedback. Successful students see feedback as a learning opportunity; a way to improve their study performance and avoid making the same mistakes again. We'll look at ways to improve your study skills and grades in Chapter 15.

5 Dedication and discipline

I have a question for you: are you studying enough to get the grades you want? If the answer is yes, then a gold star for you! If the answer is no… why do you think this is?

Perhaps you're not studying enough because you don't have a lot of time. You're combining studying with a job and everything else – family, friends, wellbeing, keeping a house, etc. If you're lacking time, you can improve this situation by making sure the time you do have is productive and focused on your most important, needle-moving study tasks.

However (and now it's time for a little tough love!) a lack of time can easily become an excuse, masking the real reason for not getting results. Dig deep and identify whether you're *truly* lacking time – or if instead you're lacking commitment and motivation. You won't be studying forever, which means at some point you will get your social life and 'me time' back. But until then, if you have decided to study – try and make it a priority in your months, weeks and days. Reconnect with your reasons for studying and commit to building study habits that allow you to give your education the focus it and you deserve.

Action steps

- Reflect on the skills you already have that will help you in your studies. What skills have you developed in your personal life, or during your career so far, that could help you in your academic journey?
- Identify which of the five independent learning skills you want to develop first.

02
Embrace your non-traditionalism as a student

A non-traditional student is someone who doesn't meet the criteria of a traditional student enrolling in full-time, campus-style study straight from school at school age. There are three common attributes of non-traditional students; some students will have one or two and some may have all three, like I did. These are:

- studying at a mature age;
- studying at a distance;
- studying while working full- or part-time.

This means that a non-traditional student – someone who has one or more of the above characteristics:

- may study part-time;
- work alongside learning;
- have taken a break from education for a number of years;
- often has conflicting priorities they need to juggle (such as a job, raising a family, volunteering, caring or more).

Essentially, a non-traditional student is fitting studying into an already busy life, rather than dedicating a number of years with a single-minded focus on studying. Non-traditional students have a unique set of needs when compared to traditional students, which means they often need a particular set of smart study strategies to ensure they get the best out of their education.

There are both advantages and disadvantages to being a non-traditional student. We'll look at some more detailed strategies in the following chapters, but you can begin to feel comfortable with your non-traditional status by understanding what those advantages and disadvantages are, and learning some tips on how to tackle them.

Mature students

A mature student is anyone over the age of 21 who delayed higher education by not going straight from school.

There are many different reasons why mature students choose to return to study. Some may have taken a few years out from education after they finished school to travel, work, or volunteer. Others may be mid-career and looking to advance their skills or change profession. Some may have taken time to raise a family and are now looking to invest in themselves and their own future. And others still may have worked for decades and be looking to try something new.

After finishing sixth form, I took four years out from education as I didn't know what I wanted to study, and I didn't think my grades were good enough to continue into higher education. Later, I decided to return to study as a mature student, because my job had sparked an interest in business and I wanted to further my career by gaining a university degree.

> **Did you know?**
>
> While it may seem like the majority of students go straight from school to higher education (especially if you're a mature student and feel like *everyone* is younger than you!), in the academic year 2016/17, approximately 59 per cent of students enrolled in higher education in the UK were aged 21 years and over (HESA, 2018). That translates to 1,367,565 students – of which 471,905 were aged 30 years and over.

Advantages of studying as a mature student
Mature students have valuable life and work experience
The knowledge and experience you gained in your years out of education will serve you throughout your studies. Depending on your subject, you may find you can use your experience to deepen your understanding of the material

and place what you're learning into a broader context. For example, a mature business student with decades of work experience may have more success in understanding and applying management theories than an 18-year-old student fresh from school.

Mature students are often more motivated to learn

Ultimately, a mature student returns to study because they want to. Choosing to study alongside an already busy life filled with work and family responsibilities is a big decision, so if you have made this decision then hold onto this foundational motivation to help you through the days where you're tired or doubting yourself.

Mature students can earn money while learning

Financial obligations such as a mortgage, rent or raising a family result in a lot of mature students needing to continue working alongside studying. Mature students don't have to put their life on hold to gain a formal qualification, and may even be in a position to pay for all or part of their education as they study, thus graduating with less or no debt – or they may even be able to ask their employer for financial sponsorship.

Mature students have useful study skills

The necessary study skills for mature students include, among others, dedication, time management and prioritization. These skills are often developed through working, volunteering and/or raising a family – which means mature students tend to have an advantage over younger students. Life and work experience help mature students understand how they like to learn and what they need to be productive and effective, which may give them a head start when they return to study.

Disadvantages of studying as a mature student

Mature students may feel isolated if they study at a traditional institution

Though there are a large number of mature students enrolling in higher education each year, their proportion at institutions tends to vary depending on the flexibility of their studying options. This may not matter for some people, but it's not uncommon for a mature student to feel lonely learning around students who are much younger than them, and who may have different interests.

> **Disadvantage busters**
>
> - Find ways to get involved at your institution, whether this is face-to-face or online. Join clubs or look for communities on social media where you can talk to other students. It can be really helpful to share your wins and struggles with students going through a similar experience.
> - If there aren't many other mature students at your institution, or you don't want to socialize with them, then make sure you lean on your own support network of friends and family to help you stay motivated, celebrate your achievements and cheer you up if you're feeling down.

Mature students fit studying around an already busy life

Overwhelm is a common side-effect of studying as a busy mature student as many will be studying alongside a whole collection of other commitments. Trying to study when you feel like you're being pulled in a million different directions is tough; there will be days when you get home late, you're tired and a little bit cranky, and the idea of dragging yourself to your desk to study feels impossible. There will be times where your course deadlines creep up way too fast and you feel like your task list is never-ending. But don't panic – this gloomy picture doesn't have to be your everyday reality. Throughout this book we'll look at a whole heap of strategies and resources you can use to help you achieve studying success, even as a busy mature student.

> **Disadvantage busters**
>
> - You must understand your workload. When you have a million other things to do each week, it can be hard to make studying a priority. Identify the suggested amount of time you should be studying each week as well as the tasks you need to complete, and use this information to plan your week.
> - Spend time at the beginning of each week deciding when you're going to study. It's easy to set an intention to study for 10 hours, but if you don't add your study sessions into your calendar, life will often get in the way and it probably won't happen.

- Mature students don't have all day to study; when time is short, it's even more important to squeeze as much value out of every study session as possible. Identify your key priorities, and don't sit down to study unless you have everything you need and have removed all distractions.

Mature students may have forgotten how to learn effectively

When it's been years since you last opened a textbook, wrote an essay or sat in an exam hall it can be daunting to start again. Your study skills probably feel a bit (or very) rusty, or you may realize you never learned how to study effectively in the first place.

There's no reason why a mature student cannot achieve grades as high as (if not higher than) a traditional, younger student. There's an old idiom that 'you can't teach an old dog new tricks'… but as Dr Vahia from Boston's McLean Hospital explains, 'New brain cell growth can happen even into late adulthood' by 'learning and acquiring new information and experiences' through formal education (Solan, 2016). This means that we *can* teach an old dog new tricks, and that returning to study as an adult can keep our brains healthy.

Disadvantage busters

- As well as spending time learning your course material, work on improving your study skills too. By buying and reading this book you have already taken the first step, so keep up the good work! By tweaking your study skills often you can affect great positive change on your grades.
- If you're not achieving the grades you want, reflect on the effectiveness of your study methods and then switch them up to meet your goals.

Distance learners

Distance learning is a method of remote education without regular face-to-face tutor contact. There are different levels of distance learning; some courses are delivered entirely online, where tutorials are virtual and communication is by forum, e-mail or telephone. Other institutions offer a blended approach with some elements, such as tutorials, delivered face-to-face.

Advantages of studying as a distance learner

Distance learning is flexible

I decided to become a distance learner because I wanted to continue working full-time. I researched the few universities near me, and none of them offered part-time courses with the flexibility I needed to continue my nine-to-five job. This is why I chose to study with The Open University, a dedicated distance-learning institution.

A large part of a distance-learning qualification is independent study, which means you can study when you want rather than having to attend lots of tutorials, workshops or lectures at set times. You're able to build your study schedule around your other commitments, such as work and family. If you're more productive in the morning, you can plan your study sessions for the early hours. Or if you're a night owl like me, and are more productive in the evenings, you can schedule in study time for when you get home from work.

Distance learners can study anywhere in the world

Distance learners have more choice about where they study; in theory, you can choose to study at any institution in the world that offers distance learning. Secondly, distance learners aren't tied to a location, therefore, throughout your studies, you can travel, or move home, without disrupting your education.

Distance learners don't have to put their life on hold

I have a friend who studies alongside home-schooling her children, a client who is completing a degree while raising her son single-handedly, and a client who qualified as a chartered accountant while working and caring for her elderly mother. Distance learners can continue their life as they study, which means achieving a qualification alongside other goals such as starting or raising a family, saving money or gaining years of valuable workplace experience.

Distance learners develop additional, valuable skills

The foundation of distance learning is independent study, which requires skills such as problem solving, self-motivation and perseverance. Studying alongside other commitments, as a lot of distance learners do, also teaches skills such as time management and prioritization. Developing these skills during your studies will help you in your future studies, career and day-to-day life.

Distance learners save time travelling to classes

As distance-learning courses consist mainly of online tutorials and independent learning, an often-substantial time saving is made by not having to travel to and from face-to-face classes. This extra time can be spent studying to achieve higher grades, or relaxing and spending time with friends and family.

Distance learners can study in comfort

I think I've left the best advantage until last. Distance learners can study from the comfort of their own homes. If you want to study on the sofa – you can. If you want to study with your cute pet as a study buddy – you can. If you want to study in your pyjamas – you can (though make sure you remember to put on some real clothes for video tutorials!).

Disadvantages of studying as a distance learner

Distance learners may struggle with the lack of social interaction

Distance learning requires students to study independently most of the time, which can be an isolating experience if you're extroverted or like to bounce ideas off other students. This can cause distance learners to procrastinate or lose motivation.

> **Disadvantage busters**
>
> - Find out if your university or college has online forums or social media groups you can get involved with. You may even be able to organize physical meet-ups in your area.
> - Study outside of the house sometimes: I love studying in cafés where the background noise and hubbub makes me feel more connected.
> - Arrange to call some of your friends during a break in a long study session, or arrange a coffee date as a break from a weekend of study.

Distance learners need to be self-motivated

At face-to-face tutorials it's easier to study alongside everyone else. Without this interaction and accountability, distance learners can struggle to stay motivated.

Disadvantage busters

- Get to know your fellow students and consider setting up an online study group for support, accountability and motivation. I regularly run 'study with me' sessions with clients where we study together on a video call. This is so helpful for distance learners who find it hard to study alone.
- Recognize and celebrate your achievements by yourself – but also with friends and family. Take the time to reflect on the hard work you're putting in, and the progress you're making, to motivate you to keep going.

Distance learners need to be confident with technology and have reliable access to the internet

Virtual tutorials, viewing materials, undertaking research, communication with your tutor and group projects are often conducted through online technologies which, to a non-techy student, can be a bit daunting. Also, without reliable, regular access to the internet, distance learning can be difficult.

Disadvantage busters

- Ask your university, college or training provider for any guides on how to use their specific technology. Many institutions have IT support, or they may even run sessions to walk you through the technology you need.
- Try to get access to a reliable internet connection so as not to interrupt your studies. This may involve you talking to or switching your internet provider, going to your local library or visiting a friend with stronger internet at times.
- If regular internet access is a problem, see if you can print resources or download them to your computer so you can study even when you're not connected.

Distance learners may struggle with the lack of direct access to their tutor

Many distance learners will never see their tutor face-to-face. This can make it more difficult to get support, feedback or additional advice from them.

Also, there's often a lag in communication between student and tutor as it's mainly conducted via e-mail. Therefore, it can take much longer to get an answer to a simple question than it would for a student at a traditional university who can go and visit their tutor face-to-face.

> **Disadvantage busters**
>
> - Build a good relationship with your tutor by introducing yourself over e-mail. When you do need to ask for help, it will be easier and you're more likely to get a helpful response.
> - Attend any and all tutorials, if you can, and engage and participate by asking questions and responding to tutor questions.
> - Start your assignments early so you have spare time to receive answers to any questions you ask.

Workplace learners

Workplace learners are students who complete a qualification alongside working in a full-time (or potentially part-time) job. Juggling work and study is a challenge, as it can be so difficult to find the time, energy or motivation to sit down at your desk after a long day at work. I completed my business degree while working full-time, so I understand the overwhelm and exhaustion this double commitment can bring.

Workplace learners decide to return to study for a range of reasons. They might want to learn new skills, progress their career, or attain a qualification so they can switch professions – or they may even be required to study (to a certain extent) by their chosen profession. I decided to go to university while working so I could pursue advancement in the company where I was working.

Advantages of studying as a workplace learner

Workplace learners earn money while learning

If you continue working while studying, you likely won't have to halt your savings plans, curb your spending or delay that new car/mortgage/dream holiday.

Workplace learners gain valuable workplace experience and skills

Lack of relevant work experience is a substantial barrier for graduates looking to enter the job market. Paradoxically, it's common to see job listings for entry-level positions with a requirement for 'X number of years of experience'.

Workplace learners increase their years of work experience as they study. Some workplace learners are able to gain experience in a career related to their chosen subject, but even if your job doesn't align perfectly, you'll still be gaining valuable experience for your future role. This could give you a head start in the recruitment process over younger, traditional graduates *without* years of work experience.

Workplace learners develop additional study skills

In most professions, companies seek employees with time management and prioritization skills. As a workplace learner, you'll naturally develop these skills as you schedule your studying into your life and manage your shifting priorities. These skills could make you more attractive to employers as well as help you succeed in your studies.

Workplace learners demonstrate grit

Deciding to study as a workplace learner *is* the more challenging route to obtaining a higher education qualification. You're sacrificing your time, energy (and a little bit of sanity!) to further yourself – which is impressive. Workplace learners demonstrate perseverance and commitment to their advancement by working hard, even when they don't feel they can keep going.

Disadvantages of studying as a workplace learner

Workplace learners have less time to study

When you already have a full-time job plus commute, a significant portion of your week is accounted for. However, workplace learners still need to find time each week to complete the required reading, note taking, activities, essays and tests. And when there are due dates looming, workplace learners often have to cut fun and relaxation from their lives, sleep less and maybe even pull a few all-nighters to get their work done.

> **Disadvantage busters**
>
> - When you have a million tasks and commitments each week it's easy to push studying to the side with, 'I'll find some time later in the week to work on my essay'. Yet, as entrepreneur Chris Ducker says, 'If it doesn't get scheduled, it doesn't get done' (Ducker, 2017). Spend 10 minutes every weekend planning your week ahead. Look at your personal and work schedule alongside your course syllabus and determine how much studying you need to do. Book these study sessions into your calendar to give yourself the best chance of completing them.
> - Work out whether you're most productive in the mornings, afternoons or evenings, and then try to flex your schedule to fit studying into these times.

Studying as a workplace learner can be stressful

Life as a workplace learner regularly threatens to overwhelm us. There will be times when you have an essay to finish at the same time as a work presentation to create, a house that needs tidying and three different appointments and events to attend. Your stress levels will rise, and you may berate yourself for your 'stupid' decision to study alongside everything else. You may start questioning your ability to do this or feel like you're letting yourself down.

> **Disadvantage busters**
>
> - Talk to your loved ones about how you're feeling. When you're doubting yourself, your support network can help pick you back up and remind you of all the ways you're incredible. If your circle's support is a little lacklustre, then don't be afraid to widen your circle. Find other workplace learners you can travel on this journey with.
> - Speak to your employer about the possibility of flexible working or offering study leave. You might be able to reduce stress and free up some study time if you can flex your work schedule at all or sometimes work from home. Alternatively, ask your employer if they'd be willing to discuss study leave – if your qualification is directly relevant to your role and could help them. I sat down with my manager and asked for study

leave by outlining how I could apply my learning to solve my team's problems. My pitch worked, and they granted me two days of study leave a month, which helped to calm my stress monster and gave me a bit more time for assignments. Maybe you don't think this is possible at your company, but it's worth an ask – focus the conversation on the benefits for them, and remember the worst thing they can say is 'no'.

Workplace learners must sacrifice their free time

As a workplace learner, you'll have to exchange some of your free time for study time. Before I started studying, as long as I had the money, I could pretty much accept any invitation for dinner, drinks or a day out. If I came home from work tired, I could collapse on the sofa and the repercussions for 'future Chloe' would be tiny. But once I became a workplace learner, 'future Chloe' got kind of peeved when I ditched the studying and decided to have fun instead because that meant 'future Chloe' had to stay up late and panic-study to catch up. Workplace learners who don't accept that their social life sometimes has to take a back seat will struggle to keep up with their workload, put themselves through a lot of stress and may complete their qualification with lower grades than they want.

Disadvantage busters

- Traditional students who don't work can afford to be inefficient with their time – but you can't. Make sure you sit down to study prepped for productivity and ready to focus.
- Plan rewards to have something to look forward to, and to motivate you to keep studying, even when you would rather have fun. Arrange a dinner, trip, fun purchase or something else that feels like a treat for after exams or big essay submissions.
- Present frustration is worthwhile for future attainment. Try to accept that 'present frustration' (studying when you would rather relax) is so worth it for the qualification and opportunities you'll gain in the future. You've decided that studying is a priority for you – so make sure the way you use your time reflects your commitment.

Workplace learners often take longer to complete their qualification

A typical undergraduate degree takes three years to complete at a full-time level of 120 credits a year. For a workplace learner studying part-time, a degree could take between four and six years or even longer. When our big goals take a long time to achieve, it's easy to lose motivation – or sometimes to not even see the point in starting them.

Disadvantage busters

- Remember the value of being a workplace learner. Though your qualification is taking longer to complete, you're achieving it alongside racking up years of workplace experience – a powerful combination.
- Before I enrolled in my degree course, I had a wobbly moment where I considered not going for it because it would take so long to achieve. Then I reminded myself that I didn't want to look back five years later and regret not starting. Time will pass anyway, so you might as well spend it working on your future and going for your dreams.

Action steps

- If you're a mature student:
  - Find opportunities to talk to and get to know other mature students.
  - Spend some time each weekend identifying your important tasks and planning your week.
- If you're a distance learner:
  - Find out what virtual and face-to-face social activities your university or college offer – and get involved.
  - Learn how to use the necessary technology in your course.
  - Introduce yourself to your tutor to build a relationship you can lean on later in your studies.

- If you're a workplace learner:
  - Work out your most productive time and schedule your study sessions into your week.
  - Speak to your employer about the possibility of study leave or flexible working.
  - Plan regular treats to keep you motivated.

03
How to prepare for higher education

Whether you're waiting to start your course or your next module, there are things you can do to hit the ground running. I remember in the few weeks before I began my degree, I was so impatient to start. My textbooks had arrived, and I'd set up my second-hand desk in my room. I was pretty nervous about returning to study, so I researched things I could do to prep for success.

Similarly, in my short breaks between modules, I was 100 per cent immersing myself in the luxury of a lot of sleep, no to-do lists and guilt-free TV binges. But I also felt a little lost because I wasn't used to having all this time off.

So I've compiled five things you can do to prepare for each module, whether it's your first or your tenth, and three tips for those who are waiting for their next module.

How to prepare for your first (or next) module

Buy some study goodies

Who doesn't love stationery shopping? I remember the sheer joy of going to town with my mum and sister during the school summer holidays to buy new supplies. I would spend ages testing all the pens and trying to persuade my mum I needed scented gel pens as well as sensible ones.

You can definitely replicate this experience for your qualification. If you want to go and buy enough stationery to start your own shop, you can! But it's not necessary, and I now recommend just buying the basics and then stocking up once you know more about the course and how you want to study.

If you choose to handwrite your notes then folders, dividers, paper, pens, sticky notes, and paperclips will be useful. As an adult I'm still a sucker for a good notebook (has to be narrow-ruled) and I am always on the look-out for the perfect ballpoint pen. If you choose to type your notes you might not need so many supplies. If you have exams in your course, then I would suggest buying some index cards too to create revision flashcards. Also, if you were thinking of investing in a new computer, laptop or tablet for your studies, then try to buy one with some time to spare, so you can set it up and get used to it before your course starts.

Plan some future fun

Starting studying for the first time, or after a break, can be overwhelming. Either you're bombarded with new demands and tasks or you've forgotten how to study over your break. I recommend planning in some fun for the first few months because if you have treats to look forward to, it will be easier to push through the days when you're lacking motivation.

Look at your calendar over the next few months and schedule in some treats; these don't have to cost a lot of money or take up a lot of time. Once you know some of your course due dates you can book in fun just after them to celebrate. Here are some ideas:

- Pre-order a novel by an author you love (who doesn't love surprise post?).
- Book a music or comedy event.
- Plan a coffee or dinner date.
- Book a massage or other treatment to pamper yourself.

Organize your time

Most learning providers give an estimate of how many hours of studying you need to complete for the course. This may be separated into taught hours (classes) and independent study. Remember though, this is only a rough guide, and you may need more or less time. Once you know the number of hours each week to aim for, you next need to work out how you're going to fit this into your schedule.

Think about when you want to study each week. Do you want to try and study every day or most days? Or would you rather study once or twice a week for longer sessions? Are there certain days of the week you're going to study? Will you try and study on days you work or on your days off?

Next, consider the time of day you would like to study. As I mentioned in Chapter 2, think about whether you have the most energy and are the most productive in the mornings, evenings or sometime in between. If you're reading this thinking, 'I'm permanently tired, so never', then picture this. It's 10 pm and you're halfway through an essay or work project that's due at midday tomorrow. Would you rather a) stay up until 3 am to finish it, or b) go to bed and get up at 5 am to work on it. If you picked 'a' you're probably a night owl and if you picked 'b' you're probably an early bird.

Get clear on how you're going to slot studying into your life and make it a priority. When your course starts, it won't be such a shock to the system – less of a slap in the face and more of a small prod in the ribs!

Create a study space you actually want to spend time in

Let's not sugarcoat the truth here – over the next few years you'll be spending *a lot* of time studying. And for a lot of you, you'll probably spend the majority of that time in the same place.

I recently polled my audience on Instagram and asked them where they like to study.

Figure 3.1 Where do you like to study?

■ In the same place   In a few different places

Figure 3.2 Where do you have your most productive study sessions?

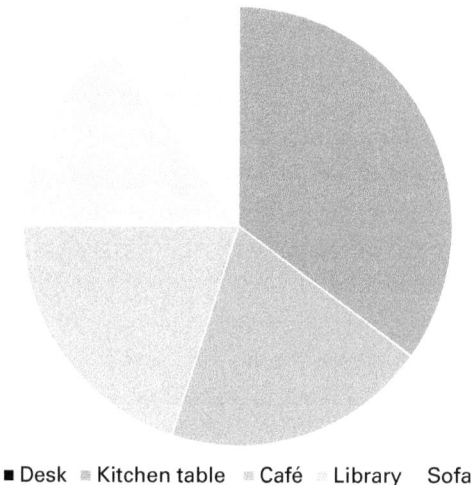

■ Desk   ■ Kitchen table   ■ Café   ■ Library   ■ Sofa

I recommend students create a desk area, even if they don't spend all their study time there, as it's great to have a dedicated study space that isn't used for relaxing or by anyone else. This isn't always possible so, wherever you study, try to turn this space into somewhere you want to be by adding things that make you happy.

For your desk you might want to add photos and posters, fairy lights or a nice lamp, candles, a comfy chair and cushions. If you're going to study at the kitchen table then you can also make this a great study space with fresh flowers, candles, and your favourite mug. If you study at a café or the library then you might want headphones, great study music and good study snacks. And finally, if you study on the sofa, then you might want a cosy blanket, candles and fresh flowers. These are the things that work for me, of course, but you get the idea – surround yourself with the things that make you feel happy and calm, and create a space where you feel comfortable.

Read through your course materials and look for additional resources

Get a feel for your course by reading through the various printed or digital materials you're sent. Try to find out: the module structure; how it will be delivered (eg online or face-to-face); how you will be assessed; and the available support services and resources. You'll also have a syllabus outlining what you'll be learning and any learning outcomes or goals you are expected to meet by the end of the module.

Look through your textbooks, and also see if there's an additional reading list you're expected to work through. It should be clear which books are mandatory and which are optional, so you may decide to buy some additional books or look for them at your local library.

Another thing you can do is engage with material outside your course. Before your module kicks off, have a look for other books, articles, magazines, podcasts or documentaries that you can consume for an introduction to the module concepts and an understanding of the context behind what you'll be studying. Before my business degree began, I bought a few copies of relevant magazines such as *The Economist* and *Inc.*, and I started looking at the business pages of my favourite news sites.

Now, here are three ways you can prepare for your next module, if you've already begun your course.

Relax and have fun

When you're used to spending every waking hour either at work or studying, it can feel very weird when you suddenly have whole stretches of time where you don't have to learn or write anything.

When you do get a break between modules, make the most of it! One thing I like to do in my study breaks is to work on non-study projects I've wanted to do for a while but haven't had the time. Have you been meaning to redecorate a room, work on the garden, or clear out your wardrobe? Now might be the time to start these, while you have the time and brain space.

The best part of study breaks for me is the recapture of my social life for a while. At busy times in my modules it feels like I'm locked away while the entire world is having fun without me, normally when it's sunny and I'm stuck at my desk as I hear children laughing and playing outside! Make the most of the time off by spending it with your friends and family who may not see you as often when you're studying. Enjoy the feeling of going out for coffee and dinner without the ever-present guilt hanging over you that you should be studying. Cook great food, bake cakes, take long baths, read a book that isn't a big, fat textbook – all the things you've wanted to do but don't have time for during study periods. Spend an evening, day, or weekend doing absolutely nothing just because you can.

Whatever you do during your study breaks, spend time with those you care about and factor in some 'me time' so you can return to study recharged and ready to kick butt.

File your study materials

You don't want to start a new module surrounded by all your old notes and documents. But your past study materials may be helpful in future modules if similar concepts are covered. Go to Chapter 7 for how to file study materials.

> **Top tip**
>
> Make sure you've downloaded anything important from your course site. For example, marked essays and tutor feedback may only be accessible for a short time once your module ends so make sure you download and print these. Having access to your past assignments and feedback is really useful when it comes to improving your study skills.

Reflect on your past performance

If you want to improve with each module, then reflection is key. The ability to reflect is an essential skill for a lot of qualifications and careers. In your studies, you may be asked to write reflective essays or journals; and in your job you'll likely be asked to reflect on your own performance during appraisals.

Before a new module, spend some time reflecting on your study abilities and performance so that you can improve and gain higher marks as you move forward. Go to Chapter 15 for a list of questions to ask yourself in preparation for your next module.

How to start each module with a bang

When you start a new module, there's information flying at you from all directions: textbooks, admin documents, e-mails and due dates. Here are the first three steps you should take to start each new module with a bang.

1 Record your important dates

As I mentioned in Chapter 1, it is your responsibility to know your due dates so that you can plan your time and ensure assignments are completed to deadline. Lots of dates will be thrown around at the beginning of your module, but more will come up as you progress, and later assessment dates are set. For example, tutorials, office hours, group projects, presentations, essays, practice tests, exams, revision sessions, etc. Go to Chapter 7 for some top tips for recording all your important dates.

2 Introduce yourself to your tutor

Even though it may feel nerdy or awkward, I want you to introduce yourself to each of your new tutors. It doesn't matter whether this is face-to-face if you study at a campus or by e-mail if you're a distance learner. Doing this starts the relationship in a positive way and demonstrates that you are interested in what they have to teach you. Introducing yourself makes a good impression and opens up a dialogue for when you have questions or need additional support throughout your module. You may also garner additional information or guidance that will help you as you study. If you choose to introduce yourself by e-mail, in some courses your tutor will send a group welcome e-mail which you can reply to, or you can just send your own.

Here are some points I recommend including in an e-mail or face-to-face discussion:

- Share what you're looking forward to learning in their module.
- Explain how this module fits into your wider study plan or career goal.
- Tell them what grades you are aiming for and ask that their assignment feedback outlines actions you can take to push your work towards these goals.
- Explain where you have study skills weaknesses and ask them for any advice they have and if they can tailor their feedback to help you improve these skills.
- Ask how and when they prefer to be contacted and what response time you should expect.
- Let them know if you have any additional needs or issues they should be aware of, for example, if English isn't your first language, you have a disability, or if you have any family or work issues that may affect your studying.

3 Organize your study materials and folders

Organization is a key skill for independent learners. It makes sense when you start a new module to spend some time collecting and organizing your various materials so you can keep important information safe and find it easily. We look at this in more detail in Chapter 7.

4 Decide on your study methods

Once you understand your module, you can start thinking about the study methods you want to try. Your study methods should be fluid: you don't want to graduate using the exact same methods you picked on your first day, as it's almost impossible that you'll immediately find the best strategies for you, that also work for all of your modules. In later chapters, we will dive deep into each of the strategies for particular types of module and assessment.

Advice for new students

Returning to study after a few years out, or a lot of years out, can be overwhelming and difficult to navigate. You probably feel like you've forgotten how to learn, or maybe like you never really knew in the first place. Maybe you're worried you won't be able to keep up with the pace, or that you're not good enough for this level of studying.

However, you won't always feel like this. As you walk through your studying journey, you will learn new skills, overcome challenges and improve your confidence as a learner. Starting anything new involves a learning curve and there will be times when you're met with resistance and doubt, and those imposter feelings may come back again. But remember this quote: 'You are braver than you believe, stronger than you seem and smarter than you think' (*Pooh's Grand Adventure: The Search for Christopher Robin*, 1997).

You made the big decision to return to study. You made the decision to bet on yourself and improve your future life through education. You also made the decision to read this book – because you're determined, and motivated to succeed. You have the power to achieve your goals.

There are many things I wish I had known before I started university that would have saved me time, energy and *a lot* of doubt-filled, teary moments. So that you can avoid making my mistakes, here are four tips for getting started and getting ahead.

Take it one step at a time

A new runner doesn't expect to run a marathon on their first outing. They start off slow and build up their training. They work up to this goal and take consistent action knowing they'll get there.

Achieving a degree or similar qualification takes a long time – so it's normal to feel disheartened at the thought of how far you have left to go. Remember, time's going to pass anyway. Thank yourself for enrolling when you did, because you'll look back and be grateful you pushed forward and worked towards your goals rather than sitting and hoping for them.

It's going to take a while to embed studying into your day-to-day life, and it will take time to carve out study time from your already busy life and work out which study techniques work for you. That's OK, because studying is a journey made up of hundreds if not thousands of steps (ie study sessions). You don't have to be a 'perfect' student for every step; what matters instead is taking consistent, imperfect action.

Don't beat yourself up if you're not jumping out of bed or racing home from work eager to sit down at your desk. Your motivation will ebb and flow and that's OK too. I would say I'm a pretty motivated person, but there have still been a shedload of times where I would whine to anyone around me that I didn't want to study and could they pretty-please do it for me?

Most importantly, be kind to yourself. If you fall behind or hit a rough patch – then that's all it is. It doesn't mean you're not good enough. Instead, pick yourself back up, remind yourself that you're kick-butt, and come up with a plan to move forwards.

Be flexible

Studying as a workplace learner, or alongside raising a family, or whatever else you have going on in your life, means you'll be pretty busy. Busy students need to be flexible to fit everything in, and to work out how they learn and study best.

As a new student, try studying at different times of the day and week, and try studying in different places too.

I always recommend having a dedicated, focused place to study – such as a desk – because you can keep your study materials at hand. But try studying too in other areas of your home, in cafés, libraries or even outside in your garden or a local park. You may discover a new favourite place to study, or just get some ideas for study spaces you can sprinkle into your routine every so often to shake up your productivity.

Respect yourself by respecting your time

There is a terrifying but necessary realization we must all have at some point – it is up to us whether we succeed in our studies (and life in general). If you choose to sleep in at the weekend or collapse on the sofa after work instead of studying... that's your decision, and you have to live with the consequences. I wish I'd known this before starting university as I often got myself into stressful situations by spending too little time studying and too much time having fun with my friends and family.

There's nothing worse than the heart palpitations and night sweats of an impending exam or essay deadline... except when you realize you brought this situation on yourself by spending too much time away from your studies.

No one wants to be the boring one who locks themselves away every evening and weekend to study. Try to accept that your social life and 'me time' is going to take a hit and you'll find it easier to deal with. Don't forget that your studying will be over at some point – so your non-existent social life won't last forever!

A common problem I hear from my clients is that their friends or family distract them or try and tempt them away from their studies. They may distract you, intentionally or unintentionally, but it's your choice whether you allow yourself to be distracted or not. There are always going to be more exciting things to do than studying, but it doesn't mean you should do them. If necessary, talk to your friends and family about the commitment you've made to your education, why you've made it and what that means for your relationships. Respect your time and others will too.

The importance of your support network

Ultimately, you are responsible for your own success in your studies. But there are things you can ask for from your support network to help you thrive rather than just survive at university.

Motivation

There will be times when you're motivated and studying feels fun and easy. But there will be other times when you'll feel like you'd rather do *anything* than sit on your butt and study (shout out to the urge to clean your bathroom when you've got an essay to write). When motivation is nonexistent, ask your loved ones to give you a pep talk to perk you back up so that you can continue. If you're feeling overwhelmed, or you've received a disappointing mark, then your friends and family can listen to you rant and moan so you can get it out of your system. They can then remind you of your reasons for doing this, and tell you that you're amazing and can conquer any challenges.

Time and space

It might be difficult at times for your loved ones to understand and support your need to study for many hours each week. Though you're the one doing the work, they have to live with the reality that you have less time and attention for them.

This may not be the case for you, but I've had a few e-mails recently from students whose families aren't very happy or are even resentful of the time they spend studying. This is a tricky topic to approach as everyone's family dynamic is different. But, ultimately, we all deserve to be supported in what's important to us. If you support your loved ones with their commitments and goals, then you should ask for this in return. Studying will have many future benefits for you and those in your circle; talk to your loved ones about your reasons for studying, so that they can get invested in your journey too. Maybe your qualification will allow you to apply for a better job with a higher salary, which means holidays and treats for your family. Maybe you'll be able to start a new career where you'll be happier and more fulfilled. Maybe you don't have a clear plan yet, but continuing education is a powerful path to take and opportunities will open up as you gain confidence and broaden your mind.

Extra support

While it would be nice if our friends and family could write our essays for us, there *are* some things they can help us with so don't be afraid to ask for extra support for the other jobs you have to fit around your studying.

If you're studying while raising children, could you ask family or friends to look after them every so often so you can have some uninterrupted study time? Or, when your workload is crazy and there are deadlines flying around, could you ask whoever you live with if they can pick up a few more chores such as cooking, washing and cleaning? Some of you may be thinking that it's not fair to ask your support network to take on more work *just* so you can study. But they're called a support network for a reason. In the same way that you support your friends and family when they need you, it's OK to ask for help in return. I regularly ask my boyfriend if he can cook more often when my workload is crazy and he agrees; partly because it makes me a happier, calmer person, but mostly because he knows once my studying has eased off I'll buy him some beers and bake him some cookies to say thank you!

Action steps

- Prepare for your *first* module and:
  - Buy some study goodies.
  - Plan in some fun treats and events now so you have things to look forward to.
  - Work out when you're going to study each week.
  - Create your perfect study space.
  - Read through your course materials.
- Prepare for your *next* module and:
  - File your previous study material.
  - Relax and have fun!
  - Reflect on your past study and identify a few actions you can take to improve moving forwards.
- Start each module with a bang and:
  - Record your important dates.
  - Introduce yourself to your tutor.
  - Organize your study materials.
- Talk to *your* loved ones about why studying is important to you, and the ways in which they can support you and your studying.

04
Goal setting

We all have a general idea of what a goal is, but we can put a slightly different spin on the idea by thinking of a 'goal' as the destination of a journey – for example, a walker might follow their local river for two hours to get to a pub.

For a student, studying towards a qualification is the journey and achieving that qualification is the destination. A lot of students set this as their only goal; their desire is to just 'get through' their studies. But you can and should set other goals too if you want to stay focused, positive and motivated throughout your long journey. You could set goals with 'legs' of your overall journey: a year of study, a specific module, or a month, week or day of work.

If you don't set study goals, you're leaving the journey – and therefore your destination – to chance. When you set a goal, you decide how the journey plays out. If you set study goals and work hard and smart to achieve them, you can achieve grades and a qualification you're incredibly proud of.

Why set study goals?

Study goal setting is important for a few reasons:

- **Focus.** You may have seen the demonstration in science class where sunlight is used to burn a piece of wood. Well, sunlight cannot burn through the material unless there is a magnifying glass to focus it. Study goals are like the magnifying glass: they give you direction and a focus for your energy.
- **Monitoring.** Setting study goals also allows you to measure your progress, and course correct if necessary. If you want to graduate with a 2:1 degree, then you might set a study goal to achieve a 60 per cent average over three years. If at the end of your second year your grade average is 55 per cent, then it's clear you need to do something, whether it's putting in more hours or switching up your methods, to increase your grades moving forward. If you didn't set the study goal, then you'd be clueless and might end up graduating with a degree you're not happy with.

- **Minimize distractions.** Reminding yourself of your study goals also helps you get back on track if you start procrastinating or responding to distractions.
- **Motivation.** A study goal gives you a clear end point, which can help keep you motivated. And setting a string of smaller study goals can help you maintain momentum through steady progress.

What study goals should I set myself?

Let's look at the two types of goals you can set and work towards.

Grade-based

A grade-based goal is an objective centred around improving assignment or exam grades. Examples of grade-based study goals include:

- achieve a 2:1 in my degree;
- achieve over 60 per cent in every essay;
- improve exam marks by 10 per cent this year;
- achieve 80 per cent in an essay by the end of the year.

Habit-based

A habit-based goal is an objective centred around forming a new habit or breaking an existing habit. Examples of habit-based forming goals include:

- practice with flashcards once a week;
- submit all assignments one day early;
- study for 30 minutes every day;
- ask or answer a question in every tutorial;
- try handwriting your notes for one month.

Examples of habit-based breaking goals include:

- spend less than 'X' hours on my phone each day;
- don't hit the snooze button on my alarm;
- don't ignore or delete tutor assignment feedback.

There are three important ingredients for study goal achievement, whether you're setting grade-based or habit-based goals: motivation, productivity and smart study strategies.

Motivation is key because there's no point setting a study goal you don't actually want to achieve. If the goal doesn't excite you (and make you a little bit nervous) you won't put in the effort needed to reach it. It's important to identify *why* you want to achieve the goal, and then keep coming back to these reasons as you work.

Productivity is the second necessary ingredient. Achieving any study goal takes time and effort; a grade-based goal requires discipline and consistent action, and a habit-based goal requires focused and productive study sessions. Later in this book we'll go through all of the productivity strategies you need to achieve your study goals.

The third key ingredient for study goal achievement is smart study strategies. You could try and dig a large hole for a week and not achieve it, no matter how hard you try, if your strategy is to use a spoon. Swap that spoon for a shovel and you'll achieve your goal in less time and with a lot less stress (and blisters!). The same principle applies to your studying. You need smart study strategies otherwise your effort is wasted. It's important to learn smart study strategies for productivity, organization, motivation, note taking, reading, essay writing and exam preparation. Luckily for you, you have this book!

Seven steps for setting epic study goals

1 *Brainstorm possible goals*

Think about the grades you're *currently* achieving, and the grades you *want* to achieve in your next module or year of studying. Note these down, and then try to think of various goals that will help you get there. An example grade-based goal could be that your current essay grades are around 50 per cent but you want to achieve 70 per cent in an essay by the end of the academic year.

Now, your habit-based goals don't have to be directly about learning – but they should be about stopping activities that hinder your studying, or starting activities that will benefit your studying. Using the same example, perhaps your study sessions are unproductive because you regularly stop working to check your phone. You could set a habit-based goal to spend less than one hour a day on social media, or to put your phone in another room every time you sit down to study.

2 Set goals and sub-goals

Once you've come up with lots of ideas, it's time to decide on your first study goals to focus on. I would recommend choosing one grade-based goal, and one habit-based goal that will help you achieve it. It's important to set goals that challenge you, but we want to also make sure they're achievable and that you believe you can meet them. To do this, split your goals into sub-goals so your focus is on a smaller and easier step to start with. Once you meet this small step, you'll feel more motivated and confident that you can push onto the next one. When I ran my first half marathon, I was terrified at the idea of running 21 kilometres. During the race, I tried not to think about the total distance but instead broke this down into the first five kilometres, then 10, then 15, then 20. This felt a lot more manageable and was how I kept my mindset positive.

If you want to achieve 70 per cent in an essay by the end of the academic year, then you will first need to increase your marks from 50 to 55 per cent, then to 60, 65, and finally to 70 per cent.

You can also split habit-based goals to make them more manageable. If you want to spend less than one hour a day on social media, for example, then you could first start with a sub-goal of spending less than three hours. Once you've achieved this, you can move onto achieving less than two hours a day, and then onto your main goal of less than one hour a day.

Try to make your first sub-goal 'easy', because a quick win will build the momentum and motivation you need to push for the scarier study goals.

3 Get motivated

If you don't feel motivated by the study goal that you're setting, you're much less likely to put in the time, effort and energy to achieve it. Grab some paper and answer the following questions about each goal.

1 Why do you want to achieve this goal? What will your studying and life look like if you achieve this goal?
2 How are you being held back by not achieving this goal?

I'll help you with an example of a study goal I set. I wanted to fit more studying into my daily routine, so I set a study goal to get to work early so that I could study for 30 to 60 minutes before my job started.

My habit-based goal that would help me achieve this was to stop hitting snooze on my alarm and just get out of bed when it sounded the first time. I wanted to achieve this goal so that I could get my important study tasks done during the week and have more free time at the weekends. Meeting this goal would mean I could arrive at work feeling refreshed and would get to the end of the day knowing I'd already completed some important study tasks.

Not achieving this goal was holding me back a lot – snoozing my alarm was making me go crazy. I wasted up to an hour every morning by hitting the snooze button so often, which made me angry because that extra time wasn't even being used for proper, replenishing sleep. This bad habit also meant I started my day off in a negative way which often impacted the rest of my day.

4 Decide on your action and strategies

Now it's time to brainstorm and decide on the actions to take to achieve your goals. Take each goal and write down possible strategies you could implement.

To improve your essay grades, you could take the following actions: start your essays two weeks before the deadline to allow enough time for reviewing; learn how to reference; use your tutor feedback to pinpoint improvement areas.

It's often necessary to clear resistance to meet your new study goals, so think about how you can prepare yourself for study goal success. For my goal to stop snoozing my alarm, I could put my phone on the other side of the room which means I have to actually get out of bed to turn it off. To improve your essay grades, you could prepare for success in the following ways: set reminders in your phone for when you need to start your essay or have a first draft; ask your friends to kick you up the butt if you don't have a first draft by 'X' date; commit to completing all your reading on time every single week.

5 Identify the support you need

It's OK to ask for help sometimes, so think about any external support you might need to help you achieve your goals.

Your tutor could help you with your essays by talking through your essay question and approach. Or you could arrange a phone call or face-to-face session to go through your latest assignment feedback and discuss where you could gain more marks next time.

Your family could help you achieve your study goals by easing the pressure in your personal life. Maybe they could help out a bit more with errands, chores or babysitting so you have more time and space to focus on your studies.

Your friends can keep you motivated and positive, and if external accountability is helpful for you, then tell them your goals and actions and ask them to check in with you on certain dates to make sure you're not slacking.

6 Plan for obstacles

You *will* face challenges as you try to achieve your study goals. Rather than letting them derail you, plan for them. Look at your goals, write down any obstacles you think you might face, and try and come up with ideas for how you can overcome them. For example, you might look ahead at your schedule and realize you've got a holiday just before one of your big essays is due. You could make a plan to work up to being one week ahead in your reading a few weeks before your holiday, block out one weekend in your schedule just for studying, and take a day's annual leave from work solely to work on your essay.

7 Pick your reward

As a busy student it's easy to move from study project to study project without looking back. It feels like as soon as you complete one assignment you need to start working on the next. Celebrate what you've achieved so you can keep your motivation high.

Think of and plan a treat for after you've achieved your study goal, or sub-goal if the timeline is long. The bigger and more challenging the goal is, the more exciting the treat should be – so that you're actually motivated to achieve it. When I got my first distinction on a module, I celebrated by going out for cocktails with some of my friends. When I realized I'd achieved First-Class Honours in my business degree, I booked a city break to Budapest with my boyfriend.

Make it happen

Setting goals is the easy part. It's fun to brainstorm new intentions, but it doesn't take too long for these good intentions to slip when the rosy glow of motivation has faded. Here are three ways to make your study goals happen.

1 Don't set too many study goals at once

It's easy to get excited about goal setting and try to work on too many at once. A great example of this is the tradition of setting New Year's resolutions. Every year I get caught up in that 'new year, new start' feeling and tell myself THIS is the year I'm going to overhaul everything.

Most years I set myself about 103 goals to: drink more water; quit sugar; meditate daily; meal prep; practise gratitude; read a novel a week; save money; study every day; sleep eight hours a night; keep my house tidy; achieve the top grade in every essay; get more flexible so I can touch my toes; learn Spanish… the list goes on and on… and on.

I feel motivated and eager on January 1st, but a week later I've achieved nothing but feeling a little more hydrated and a lot more rubbish about myself. I want to give you (and me!) permission to take it easy on the goal setting. Instead of setting a million goals, or even five, pick a maximum of one grade-based and one habit-based goal to focus on right now. If your progress is good in four to six weeks, then consider adding in one more.

Keeping your number of study goals lower will help you stay focused and stop you chasing every shiny object. The way to create long-term change, which is where the good stuff happens, is through manageable, sustainable progress.

2 Track your progress

If you don't track your progress, then you won't know when you've met your goal or whether you need to adjust your strategies. When you track your study goals, you get the added benefit of increased motivation because you can see the progress you're making.

There are lots of different ways you can track goals depending on the type of goal and your personal preferences. If you're trying to set a daily habit, such as not hitting the snooze button, or studying for 10 minutes, then you could try using the Seinfeld method. Comedian Jerry Seinfeld has a method for getting better at writing jokes (Trapani, 2007). He uses a big wall calendar and every day that he writes jokes he puts a big red cross through that day. Jerry's job then is to not break the chain. As the chain grows, you'll like seeing your progress and you won't want to miss a day. If your habit-based goal is weekly, such as creating flashcards for revision, then you could alter this method slightly and create a poster separated into weeks, not days. Each X marks a week when you completed your goal activity.

For grade-based goals, I'd recommend creating your own tracker. You could create a poster with your goal listed at the top. Then add a table with your assignments in one column and the marks you achieve in another column. As you progress through your module(s) you'll be able to see your marks (hopefully) increase towards your goal.

There are plenty of habit-tracking apps you can download too, some paid and some free. I've used a free app called Habit-Bull before, which is a great way of tracking your study goals and any personal goals you have too. You simply add in your goals and the details of when and how often you want to work towards them. Then, you check off the activity every time you complete it and watch your progress.

3 Reflect and don't be afraid to pivot

Unfortunately, we can't just set and forget our study goals. The act of deciding on a goal doesn't mean you will achieve it; but also, if you find you're not making the progress you want, it's essential to reflect on whether your methods are working. A saying I remind myself of often is: be stubborn about your goals and flexible about your methods. The outcome of your goal, the destination, is what's important, so don't be too precious about how you get there.

Earlier this year I wanted to lose weight, so I started running twice a week. After a month or so I was pretty peeved to find I'd barely lost anything. I started doubting whether I could even achieve this goal and I just wanted to give up. But then I remembered to get flexible with my methods. I added a few lunchtime walks to my routine and I started counting my calories. Within a week I had noticed a difference and my motivation to keep working on my goal was increased.

Commit to reviewing your study goals often. You want to identify your progress and whether your methods are working. Add regular reminders in your calendar to reflect on your study goals by asking yourself the following questions:

1 What is going well? What benefits have you achieved so far?
2 What have you struggled with? What challenges have you faced?
3 What could you do differently? What new strategies could you try?

And if you've met your goal or sub-goal…

4 What are your next steps?

> **Action steps**
>
> - Brainstorm and then decide on one grade-based and one habit-based study goal.
> - Split these into sub-goals and identify the strategies and actions you'll take to achieve them.
> - Ask for support, plan for any possible obstacles and pick a reward for when you achieve each goal.
> - Decide how you're going to track your progress and reflect often on the effectiveness of the strategies you're using.

Part Two
Mindset and motivation

05
Mindset

Do you ever think these things when you're studying?

- I'm just not that smart.
- I don't get this at all.
- This is too hard, I want to give up.
- I can't improve.
- You're either good at studying or you're not – and I'm not.

These statements originate from a fixed mindset, which Stanford Psychology Professor Carol Dweck explains is the belief that intelligence is unchangeable (Dweck, 2017). Your intelligence is fixed, so some people are smart and some people aren't. On the other hand, growth mindset is the belief that intelligence is malleable, that it can be developed. Students with a growth mindset believe they can become more intelligent with hard work, perseverance, self-belief and the right study strategies.

Carol Dweck and her co-authors, Lisa Blackwell and Kali Trzesniewski, conducted two studies in a New York junior high school to discover the impact of students' beliefs around intelligence on their maths scores (Blackwell et al, 2007). The first study followed four waves of students over two years from when they started seventh grade (aged between 12 and 13). The 373 students were asked to complete questionnaires on their beliefs and motivations around intelligence, effort and academic achievement. From this they determined whether each student exhibited a fixed mindset or a growth mindset. At first, there wasn't much difference between the maths scores of the two groups. But by measuring their progress and grades over seventh and eighth grade, they found a link between beliefs around achievement and actual grades achieved. Overall, the students with a growth mindset increased their scores compared to the fixed mindset students whose scores plateaued or even decreased.

A second study was conducted to see if teaching students that their intelligence can be increased would see an actual improvement. They took 99 lower-ability students, split them into two groups of equal academic achievement and assigned them to an eight-week intervention project after school. Both groups were taught study skills and how the brain works. But one group were also given lessons on growth mindset and how you can grow your intelligence and become smarter through learning. Both groups were on a declining grade trajectory – their grades were predicted to continue falling. However, after the intervention class, the growth mindset group reversed this trajectory and their grades increased, whereas the grades of the group who were only taught study skills continued to decline.

The group who were taught their intelligence was malleable became empowered and motivated to learn because they believed effort would make them smarter and increase their grades. One boy, who was known as a troublemaker, had tears in his eyes as he said to the researcher, 'You mean, I don't have to be dumb?' (Trei, 2007).

Labelling yourself as a bad student with low intelligence limits you and your ability. If you think you're a C-grade student then that's what you'll stay, or you might even become a D-grade or E-grade student. If you don't believe you can achieve high grades, then you won't feel motivated to learn and you won't see the point in putting in the work to achieve them. This acts as a self-fulfilling prophecy allowing your make-believe limits to become concrete ones.

Talent vs hard work

The idea that our intelligence is not static is an odd one to get your head around, because at school, many of us are made to believe that natural talent is the key to academic success. We're tested on our natural intelligence and abilities from an early age, and these scores are used to categorize us based on our 'potential'. The problem is that we're labelled without taking into account our effort and hard work, and before we're taught smart study strategies that help us unlock our potential. Natural talent is often pushed as the key ingredient of academic achievement, and if teachers and schools decide that you don't have enough of it, then you can be made to believe that academic success is unlikely for you, and that perhaps you should apply yourself to something less academic.

This is a load of hooey, frankly, because really, what is talent? To be called talented means someone thinks that one day you could be really good at something. Talent refers to potential rather than actual success. Everyone is talented in something, but not everyone is successful. Why? Because talent is *not* the most important ingredient of success. Hard work and effort are *way* more vital. Author Stephen King (1981) is quoted in his non-fiction book *Danse Macabre* as saying, 'Talent is... cheaper than table salt. What separates the talented individual from the successful one is a lot of hard work and study: a constant process of honing.'

When I moved into sixth form aged 16, I thought I would sail through. I'd been labelled bright and clever my entire life – I was even put onto a 'gifted and talented list' at school. But what actually happened was I failed my first exams, dropped out of my physics class, was almost kicked out of my maths class, and left two years later with crappy grades and even crappier self-esteem. I'd never had to try before, so I didn't bother! It took a few years of feeling like I was stupid before I learned the power and value of hard work.

Self-discipline matters more than IQ

A study by Angela Duckworth and Martin E P Seligman investigated the impact of self-discipline compared to IQ on the grades of 13–14-year-olds (Duckworth and Seligman, 2005). For the first group of students, self-discipline was measured using parent and teacher reports and a questionnaire regarding their impulsivity and ability to delay instant gratification. The second group were also asked to complete an IQ test.

The study found that self-disciplined students procrastinated less and spent longer on their homework than their more impulsive peers. This hard work and effort were worth it because these students achieved higher grades and more easily gained admission to competitive high schools. Self-discipline as a measurement accounted for more than twice as much variance as IQ when it came to final grades and hours spent studying. In other words, students with high self-discipline outperformed those with low self-discipline – even if they were of the same intellectual ability.

Here are two of my favourite examples of people who've demonstrated a growth mindset and the notion that hard work is more important than talent. Basketball star Michael Jordan was dropped from his high school basketball team for being too short (Newsweek, 2015). Rather than simply accepting it, he worked hard to improve. Whenever he was tired and wanted to stop, '…I'd close my eyes and see that list in the locker room without my name on it', which fired him up to keep pushing. The next year he made the varsity squad, and the rest is history.

Author J K Rowling was famously turned down by 12 publishers before the 13th agreed to publish the first Harry Potter book (Oswald, 2016). Many of the publishers gave her negative feedback, but her self-belief that she had a story people would read spurred her on. The same thing happened *again* when she tried to get published under a pseudonym for a new series of books. Rather than see rejections as failures, Joanna kept pushing (Rowling, 2016). She said, 'I wasn't going to give up until every single publisher turned me down, but I often feared that would happen.'

If you ever feel held back by your own perceived lack of natural talent, direct your energy instead towards working hard and developing a growth mindset so you can push past the limits you and others have put on yourself.

Fixed vs growth mindset

To better understand growth mindset, it's useful to look at the differences between a fixed and growth mindset.

> *Students with a fixed mindset give up when things get tough, whereas students with a growth mindset persevere and overcome setbacks.*

When I was 17, just a few months into year 11 at sixth form, I took my first physics exam and failed with 22 per cent. Brilliant. My tutor asked to see me and explained that I would need to work a lot harder if I wanted to do well in this subject. Back then, my fixed mindset was *strong*. I thought that if I had to work hard then I couldn't be that good, so I quit. I dropped out of that class rather than do the work. If I'd had a growth mindset, I would have seen this failed exam as a challenge and a learning opportunity.

> *Students with a fixed mindset seek to look smart, whereas students with a growth mindset seek to learn.*

Fixed mindset students are unlikely to try new things for fear of failure. A year after I completed my business degree, I decided to enrol in a creative writing course, but I was terrified. I had achieved a First-Class degree, so I'd enjoyed the feeling of *finally* being academically successful. The idea of starting a new subject was scary because I might not be any good. My old friend Fixed Mindset had returned. I didn't want to go back to that crappy time in my life where I didn't believe in myself and my ability to learn. And, I'd started a business based around me being a successful student! When these doubts struck, I recognized them as being part of a fixed mindset, so I tried to flip it and do the growth mindset thing. A student with a growth mindset tries new things because they want to learn and they're not afraid of failure because they know it's necessary to become good at something.

> *Students with a fixed mindset ignore feedback and constructive criticism, whereas students with a growth mindset seek feedback and use it as an opportunity to improve.*

No student wants to receive negative feedback. Even though we know it's 'constructive' (said with a large eye roll) it feels pretty *destructive* to our self-esteem. Students with a fixed mindset either don't look at their feedback, glance over it then ignore it, or get super upset and struggle to push forward at all. But it's important to develop a growth mindset so we can make the most out of the feedback we're given at university or college. Soon into my degree I developed a system for taking my tutor feedback and using it to gain more marks with every essay – take that, Fixed Mindset!

How can I develop a growth mindset?

You're never too far down your path to stop, pivot and change your route. Believe you can become smarter, and you're already halfway there. Here are three simple but powerful ways to develop a growth mindset.

Mistakes are necessary for success

Getting a low score on an essay sucks. Running out of time in an exam hurts. But what hurts the most is making the same mistake again. Mistakes in our studying happen, and that is 100 per cent OK. They happen when we're pushing ourselves and learning something new. Making a mistake is fine, but the *failure* is if you don't learn from it and make the same mistake again unnecessarily. For example, let's say you lose five marks in an essay because you didn't reference/cite properly. You get this feedback and do nothing with it, so you lose another five marks in your next essay. This is where the failure occurs, because you could have learned from the mistake and achieved five more marks by finding out how to reference accurately.

No one likes hearing or reading negative feedback, especially if you felt happy with your studying performance. Accepting mistakes is difficult because they are often wrapped up in emotions of guilt, embarrassment or 'not-enoughness'. Try not to fear mistakes but instead see them as opportunities to improve. Remember, the expert in anything was once the beginner.

Look out for examples of people who've made missteps and come back stronger, and you'll find it easier to bounce back and learn from your own mistakes. Once you get over the sting of a setback, reflect on what went wrong and what you could do differently next time.

When you build a habit of learning from feedback and mistakes, errors can actually be a way of accelerating your achievement, because they give you an opportunity to work on your weaker areas, improve and achieve higher marks with every assignment or exam.

Put on your persevering pants

Students with a fixed mindset believe failure results from low ability; so if you fail, you might as well give up. When I failed my first physics exam, I didn't see the point in trying again. Surely you can't be very good at something if you need to put in a lot of effort? On the other hand, students with a growth mindset believe failure results from not putting in enough effort, or from using the wrong strategy. This means that if we want to become smarter and achieve higher grades we have to put in more effort.

Now this doesn't mean you have to study every hour of the day, it instead means you need to increase your productivity but also your perseverance. It's the growth mindset ability to keep plugging away that leads to academic achievement.

Try to focus on your effort rather than your outcomes. When you submit essays, are they your best work or simply 'good enough'? If you submit essays because you can't be bothered to do any more or because you run out of time, then your effort may be holding you back from higher grades. Sometimes life happens and you can't do your best work 100 per cent of the time, but what about aiming for 90 per cent, or 95? Aim to always submit work you're proud of, and your hard work and persistence will pay off in increased intelligence and better results.

Be inspired and learn from successful people

There are very few people who've become successful by chance or by sitting back and relaxing. It's like an iceberg. Above the water we see someone's achievements. But below the water is where most of the iceberg lies: the dedication, hard work, challenges, mistakes, and learning they've been through to get to success.

Instead of feeling jealous or writing off your own success because you don't have their luck/support/whatever, be inspired by others and the path they've walked to get where they are. See what you can learn from them to help you on your path.

Watch TED talks and documentaries, listen to podcasts and read autobiographies about people working hard to achieve incredible things. Here are some of my favourite examples of growth mindset in action:

- *The Climb* (Froome, 2014) is an autobiography by professional road racing cyclist Chris Froome. Even if you don't like or know a lot about cycling, this book has a lot of lessons. It details the obstacles and hard work Chris endured to get to his success today, and it definitely gave me a kick up the butt to study harder. It also taught me that it doesn't matter how many times you get knocked down (quite literally in Chris's case) as long as you get back up.
- Episode #174 of *The Tim Ferriss Show* podcast (Ferriss, 2016) features an interview with Nicholas McCarthy, a successful concert pianist with only one hand. He taught himself to read music and play the piano even though he had a lot of doubters. At age 16, he applied for a music school and was turned down because the teacher didn't want to make the time for someone who couldn't play two-handed. Nicholas didn't let this stop him. He worked hard and has since graduated from the Royal College of Music in London, played alongside Coldplay and all around the world.
- The TED talk *Kids Can Teach Themselves* by Sugata Mitra (2007). He talks about his Hole in the Wall project where computers were 'mysteriously' left in very remote Indian villages. The project observed local children who had never seen a computer before, learn how to use them and then began teaching others. This is a great talk to make you believe in your own capacity for learning. No more feeling bad because you don't understand a concept yet.

These are the things that work for me, but you can find the people who inspire you in all sorts of places. Add inspirational content to your day-to-day life, because when you surround yourself with examples of growth mindset, your own possibilities start to expand until you believe you can become smarter yourself.

Mindset gremlins

Now we've talked about the yay parade that is growth mindset, it's time to talk about the not-so-fun stuff – our mindset gremlins. These are parts of your brain that try to protect you from danger, failure or embarrassment, but in the context of studying, could well be holding you back from achieving what you want. Here are the three common symptoms of what I like to call Mindset Gremlin-itis.

Low motivation

When negative self-talk kicks in and you start doubting yourself and your abilities, your motivation to study is going to be damaged, as you won't see the point in studying. If you don't think you're capable of getting the work done, or achieving a good grade, then you won't put in the effort needed.

Procrastination

When you're scared of failure, have a hard task in front of you, or you can't see the light at the end of your studying tunnel, your brain will try to protect you by tempting you to procrastinate. Your brain doesn't want to feel uncomfortable so when faced with a hard or scary task it will try and persuade you to do something easier instead, like clean the bathroom or watch hours of YouTube.

Self-sabotage

Some of us add even more fuel to the fire by consciously or unconsciously damaging our progress and success. If you try really hard on an essay and score a low mark then you'll feel like there's no hope, right? Your dreams will be dashed, and you'll finally have the proof you need that you're a bad student. You might put off studying until it's too late to do the job well because it's nicer for your brain to tell itself that you got a low mark because you didn't try. Sometimes it's easier to do badly kind of on purpose, because then you have an excuse for it rather than having to accept you're not good enough.

I'm going to walk you through the five common, study-success-restricting mindset gremlins – and how to muzzle them.

Imposter syndrome

Imposter syndrome is a collection of feelings of inadequacy where 'imposters' experience chronic self-doubt about their abilities, despite evidence, occasional feelings of success and compliments from others – they feel like a fraud who's going to be found out. This is particularly relevant for those of us who return to study, because our years out may make us feel like we've forgotten how to learn or like everyone else is going to be better or faster than us (#nottrue).

Imposter feelings can be further exacerbated by what I call education scars, the long-lasting imprints of a bad past study experience. A student may have education scars if they've experienced failure or bad grades before or if they were dismissed as not being smart or academic by parents, teachers or siblings.

These education scars can stay with you for a long time. Even when they're faded, they can still show up in the right light as imposter syndrome. I definitely struggled with imposter syndrome throughout my degree. Every time I hit a challenge my doubts would rear up and I'd be hit by bad memories from sixth form, like being told I wasn't a good student, and being dismissed from career workshops because I wasn't going to university. Imposter syndrome blinds you to your strengths and the good stuff that's happening in your studies until you're just left doubting yourself.

But there are steps we can take to overcome imposter syndrome:

- **Recognize imposter feelings** as they emerge. Acknowledging them as 'imposters' distances them from you and takes away some of their power.
- **Remind yourself** that these feelings are normal and are simply a response to the challenging environment you're now in. Pushing ourselves is necessary for growth but it's uncomfortable and our brains don't like it so it's easier to nip your growth in the bud with imposter thoughts than allow yourself to make mistakes and risk failure, disappointment or embarrassment.
- **Talk about your feelings.** Sometimes we can get stuck in our own heads and think we're the only one going through a crap time. But reach out to the people who care about you and talk to them about what you're experiencing. Start conversations with your network around fears and doubts and you'll be able to a) recognize that everyone feels like an imposter at times, and b) support each other in quietening your imposter thoughts.

I'm a bad student

Guilt and shame are fairly common emotions when you're a student. If you're like me, you've felt guilty when you've not studied when you said you would, or you took an evening, day or week off of studying, or you procrastinated over your essay and submitted it *just* in the nick of time. This guilt can sometimes turn into shame where you believe you're lazy because you don't study enough, or that you're a bad student because you can't stay focused for longer than 10 minutes or achieve more than 'X' per cent in an essay or exam.

Regularly feeling guilty for your studying behaviour can lead into a lovely spiral of negativity and the conviction that you're a bad student.

Here are some ways to overcome this gremlin:

- **Change your language**. Try not to refer to yourself as a bad student. Believing you're inherently bad at anything is going to limit your success, as you'll end up turning these thoughts into reality. If you catch yourself thinking or saying, 'I'm a bad student', replace this with something more freeing such as, 'I don't feel good about my studying right now but I believe in my ability to turn this around.'
- **Reframe** what being a good student means. Here's what a 'good student' *doesn't have to* mean:
  - all you do is study in every possible moment;
  - you achieve top grades in every assignment and exam;
  - you have to be 100 per cent efficient every second of the day.

  Instead, here's what being a 'good student' *should* mean:
  - you work hard and keep going when you hit challenges;
  - you make progress on your goals, even if the steps are tiny and imperfect;
  - you pull back at times, rest and look after yourself.

We seem to equate being a good student as being a perfect student. Well, this is baloney – because there's no such thing as a perfect student! I'm not a perfect student, and I still achieved a First-Class degree while working full time. I say this not to brag, but to demonstrate that success in life is not about being perfect. Study success comes from keeping a positive, growth mindset, working hard and using the right study strategies.

Fear of failure

Fear is a deeply embedded, fundamental reaction to protect us from threats. Our ancestors needed fear to protect them from predators. But running away from lions is not something most of us have to worry about today. Fear can be a response to an actual danger or it can be self-created, such as fear of the dark or fear of achieving a low grade or falling behind with your workload.

In the months before my first university exam I put off starting my revision because I didn't want to realize that I didn't know or remember anything. This fear held me back from doing the work needed to prove the fear false. Instead of beginning revision early, I put it off and put it off until finally I didn't have enough time to do it well. In the exam I wasn't able to perform at my best but that was OK because 'Ahah!' – I proved my fear right! I achieved a lower grade than I wanted, which made me believe my fear was rational. I was able to confirm my story that I couldn't do well in exams.

It wasn't until the next year, when I'd dedicated time to improving my mindset, that I realized this pattern was unhelpful.

Here are some ways to tame this gremlin:

- **Rationalize the situation.** What does the evidence say? Are you likely to fail your exam when you've achieved good marks in all the others?
- **Imagine the worst-case scenario.** This is a scary prospect, but often you'll realize it's not as bad as you think. Doing this can also help you plan for this possible scenario. If you're really worried about an upcoming exam, for example, ask your tutor what support is available to help you increase your chance of passing.
- **Visualize the best-case scenario.** What will happen if you do well? Picture this clearly and richly and focus on what you feel. For exams, imagine yourself walking out of your exam with your head held high or celebrating when you find out your grade. For essays, imagine the satisfaction of submitting something you're proud of and how incredible your graduation will be.
- **Feel the fear and do it anyway.** Courage doesn't mean the absence of fear, it means moving forward and doing the thing *despite* the fear. Being scared isn't a reason to not try. Remind yourself that the best things in life, the stuff you really want, are on the other side of fear.

Negative thinking

Psychologist and author Rick Hanson talks about the phenomenon of the negativity bias (Hanson, 2010). This is our predisposition to notice the bad stuff that happens to us more easily than the good stuff. As we've evolved over millions of years, Rick says we've learned to dodge sticks such as predators or natural disasters, and chase carrots such as food. It was more important to notice and react to sticks than carrots because missing out on some berries wasn't permanent (there would be another chance at finding some) whereas failing to avoid a lion or a violent outburst from another human meant game over and no chance to pass on their genes.

Thankfully, life today is pretty different, but our negativity bias still exists. Hanson says 'The brain is like Velcro for negative experiences, but Teflon for positive ones' (Hanson, 2010). This means that good grades, positive feedback and productive study sessions are likely to slide off our conscious (like the non-stick pan coating, Teflon), whereas we absorb the negative things that happen to us. When we don't meet our study goals or we receive negative feedback – this stuff sticks, so we have to work a lot harder to shake it off.

If we receive a low grade in an essay or exam, this one negative event becomes mammoth in our mind, crowding out memories of good stuff that's happened. I remember a time in English class at school where I was maybe 13 or 14. Our teacher asked a question and I put my hand up to answer like the Hermione Granger wannabe I was (and still am sometimes). She picked me and I gave my answer. I can't even remember what my answer was but I remember her response. 'No,' she said with a scoff and an eyeroll, 'of course that's not right.' She immediately turned away and asked someone else for the answer. For such a small moment in my life this sure stuck with me. Even now, there are times when I'm hesitant to put up my hand in a tutorial and offer an answer because of that moment. It doesn't matter that there have been 100 times where I've got an answer right and received praise and a smile – it's the one negative time that sticks.

To tackle the negative thinking gremlin:

- **Name your inner critic.** One thing I do and recommend is to give your negative inner critic a name. Come up with a silly name like Negative Nancy, Gremlin, the Perfectionist or Nag to help you break out of the negative pattern. It's hard to take your destructive self-talk seriously when you name it something silly. I call my inner critic Muggle, and when I notice I'm slipping into negative thinking I call it out, thank it for protecting me then tell it to move along. I say, 'I see you Muggle. Thank

you for trying to protect me but I don't need you. I've got studying to do so leave me alone.' Try this and you'll find it easier over time to distance yourself from your negative inner critic's influence.
- **Track your achievements.** Over time, this positive activity will disrupt and break your negative pattern. You could spend a minute at the end of each study session noting down the things you've completed and any wins. At the end of the day you'll be able to smile at the progress (however small) you've made.

I've failed so what's the point?

Study mistakes or failed/low grades, whether expected or unexpected, make you feel like you've been winded. But as we learned earlier, mistakes are necessary for growth. Misreading an essay question is going to teach you next time to make sure you understand the question before you start writing. Misjudging your exam timings will teach you to plan out your time in future exams. But the only way we can learn these lessons and improve next time is if we pick ourselves up and try again, even if we don't want to.

Here are two ways you can overcome this gremlin:

- When you're ready, **reflect** on what happened. If you need some help with this, you could ask your tutor for their input. Identify your improvement areas and create a plan to work on these moving forward. Small tweaks to the way you study can have really big results for your grades. I've worked with clients who jumped entire grades just by learning some smarter study techniques.
- Try to **distance yourself** from this mindset gremlin by not letting your thoughts become permanent. Maybe you feel like you've failed, but that doesn't mean that *you* are a failure. You're a hard-working student challenging yourself to push past your setbacks. Reconnect to the reasons why you're studying and what you want to do with your qualification.

The power of positivity

Setbacks are a normal part of studying, whether it's achieving a low grade, getting criticism from your tutor, not understanding a key concept, falling behind or not knowing how to note take/write an essay/revise, etc. Positivity is a powerful emotion and attribute, because it helps you overcome these challenges, as well as increasing your motivation and drive to keep pushing towards your ultimate study goal of achieving your qualification.

We learned earlier that our brain settles into negativity more easily than positivity, but we can break out of this pattern and build a new one because we can develop positivity, like a muscle. There are ways we can increase this emotion in our studying and build a happier habit. Imagine what you could achieve if you felt positive about your studying.

Harness the power of your words

The way you talk to yourself is powerful, but it can be powerful in a good way or a bad way.

When you're having a tough study day and feel like nothing's going right it's easy for these thoughts to creep in and take hold. But we can't let that happen, because negative self-talk destroys your motivation and allows room on your shoulder for your negativity gremlin.

What we need to do is transform our thinking. If you catch yourself thinking or saying something negative about your abilities, or even about who you are as a person, flip your words into positive self-talk to keep your happiness and motivation high.

Changing a few words may seem a little trivial but over time the thoughts you tell yourself become your truth. Altering your thoughts will allow you to steer yourself into a more positive frame of mind.

Look for the green lights

There are days on my commute to and from work where it feels like every traffic light I meet is red. The journey feels longer and more stressful as I'm

Figure 5.1 Reframe your words

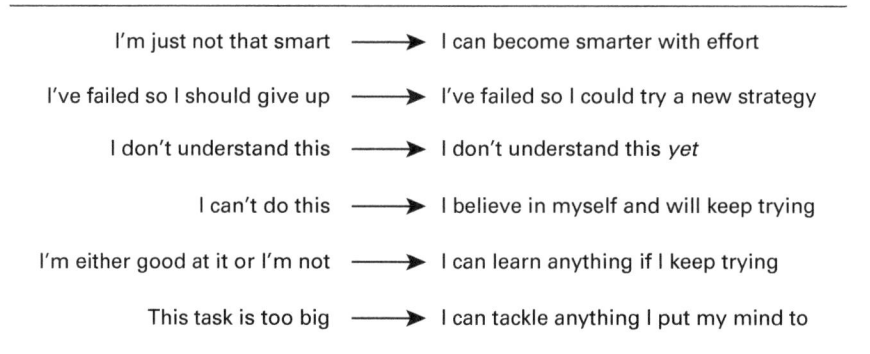

I'm just not that smart	⟶	I can become smarter with effort
I've failed so I should give up	⟶	I've failed so I could try a new strategy
I don't understand this	⟶	I don't understand this *yet*
I can't do this	⟶	I believe in myself and will keep trying
I'm either good at it or I'm not	⟶	I can learn anything if I keep trying
This task is too big	⟶	I can tackle anything I put my mind to

hit with red light after red light. This is how I've felt in my studying at times too. I come across difficult concepts, tricky assignment questions and boring readings. It's easy to feel negative when it seems like everything is a red light.

But that's not true. Sometimes our brain gets stuck in a pattern of noticing red lights. If you notice one red light, you're more likely to notice another, and soon you're looking out for them. On my commute there are red lights but there are also green lights, other drivers who let me out, pedestrians that say thank you when they cross, and cute puppies trotting down the road.

In my studying I come across problems, yes. But there are also times when I get good feedback on an assignment, get into the flow of writing easily, understand a concept quickly or just write a really great set of clear notes. Sometimes we have to remove our negative glasses so we can see how many positives are around us. At times we have to specifically look for the good stuff that's happening in our studying and our days.

One of my favourite quotes is said by Dumbledore to Harry in *Harry Potter and the Prisoner of Azkaban*: 'Happiness can be found even in the darkest of times, if one only remembers to turn on the light' (Rowling, 1999). I love this simple reminder that, even if we don't have control over what happens to us and the challenges we face in our studies, we *do* have control over how we feel about these struggles.

To be more positive, and to reap the benefits of this in your studying, stop looking for the things that go wrong and start looking for the things that go right instead. One way to do this is to practice gratitude. There are specific gratitude journals you can buy, or you could simply add it into any other planning or journaling activity. Each day, note down one or more things you're grateful for. Even on the worst day ever you can think of something you're grateful for – like the day earlier this year when I was miserable and laid up with the flu. I could have thought about how awful I felt, and how grumpy I was, but instead I chose to write in my planner that I was grateful for my health. I was grateful my sickness was only temporary, when so many others have to cope with illness every day. Practising gratitude shifts your thinking and over time you will find it easier to feel positive.

If you're struggling to find positives in your studying, start by recording the green lights in your day-to-day life first. A recent green light for me was when I visited a different site for work. I bought one chocolate bar from the vending machine and two fell out – #winning!

Allow the joy in

I'm a big believer in finding the joy in your day. Cracking a smile or belly laughing until it hurts is vital for your happiness, and when you're happy, you'll find it a lot easier to study.

I want you to actively look for more ways to allow the joy into your day. One thing I do to allow the joy in is queue up some funny YouTube videos to watch in my study breaks. I love interview clips from talk shows and comedy shows. I also follow certain accounts on Instagram that make me smile – any with funny illustrations or by people who rescue or look after animals. Another thing that gives me joy at the moment is video calling my nephew. He's two years old so is at that adorable stage where he understands everything and laughs all the time.

Work out what makes you smile and laugh and find times for it in your day – even if it's just for five minutes before you study and in your breaks. Your mood will lift and your studying, future success and everyone around you will thank you for it.

Action steps

- Reflect on whether you currently have a fixed or growth mindset.
- Think of someone famous or that you know who has overcome challenges to achieve success. What can you learn from them?
- Make a list of people that inspire you to be a better student and person.
- Identify your most common mindset gremlin and take one action to begin taming it.
- Make a list of the things that give you joy and add more of them into your day.

06
Motivation

A key ingredient for successful studying and achievement of goals is motivation – having a strong reason to act or accomplish something. In studying, you need motivation to compel you into doing the work to complete your qualification with the grades you want, but sometimes it's pretty elusive. One day you're eager and raring to get to it, but other days it seems impossible to muster any enthusiasm to open your books, and you'd much rather watch back-to-back episodes of your favourite TV show. You'll probably find you're more motivated at the beginning of your studying journey, or at the start of each new module. But it takes a *long* time to complete a degree or similar higher education qualification... so your enthusiastic attitude won't last long unless you build sustainable study motivation.

In my experience, there are two types of studying motivation, and both of them are necessary to get and stay motivated throughout your entire qualification.

One-day motivation

First, we have one day study motivation. This is the type that's most talked about, and it involves motivating yourself in the present by looking forward to the future. You'll use your future dreams to compel you to study towards them now.

> ### Try this – what is your one-day motivation?
>
> To identify your one-day study motivation, ask yourself the following questions, then note them down or turn them into a mind map on one half of a piece of paper.
>
> - Why did you start studying?
> - What do you want to do with your qualification?

- What is your long-term dream for your education?
- Are you studying to prove something to yourself?
- Are you studying for someone (eg your children) or in memory of someone?

Figure 6.1 My one-day motivation example

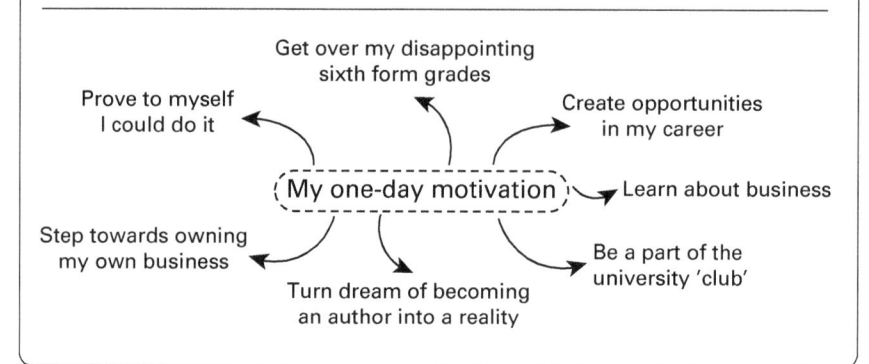

```
                  Get over my disappointing
                       sixth form grades
   Prove to myself                              Create opportunities
     I could do it                                  in my career
                        My one-day motivation        Learn about business
   Step towards owning
    my own business                              Be a part of the
                                                 university 'club'
                       Turn dream of becoming
                       an author into a reality
```

Everyday motivation

Some students find it fairly easy to go through present frustration (studying now) for future success (academic achievement). But a lot of students need more tangible study motivation to make them work now. Everyday motivation isn't talked about anywhere near as much, but I think it's key when you're working towards a longer-term goal. Yes, you need to have an idea what you want in your future, but when your graduation is far away you might need some motivation that's a little closer to home.

Everyday motivation refers to the small, day-to-day things that help you enjoy and get through your study sessions.

Try this – everyday motivation

To work out your everyday study motivation, answer this question: what little things motivate you to learn and work hard every day? Use the list of my examples to get started with some ideas, and write your answers on the second half of your piece of paper.

Figure 6.2 My everyday motivation example

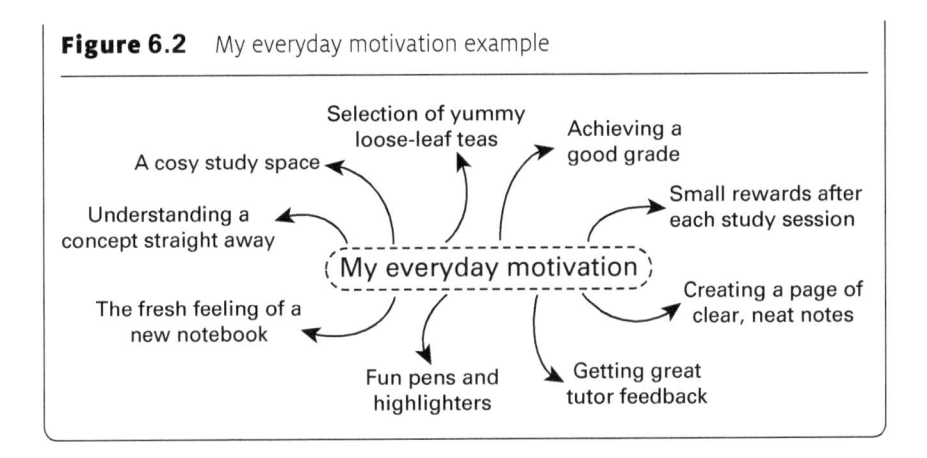

- A cosy study space
- Selection of yummy loose-leaf teas
- Achieving a good grade
- Small rewards after each study session
- Understanding a concept straight away
- My everyday motivation
- Creating a page of clear, neat notes
- The fresh feeling of a new notebook
- Fun pens and highlighters
- Getting great tutor feedback

Pin your lists to your wall, or keep them in your folder, so that you can see them often, and whenever you're feeling unmotivated take a look at them. Reconnect to your longer-term reasons for studying, then check whether your day-to-day studying includes the things that help you stay motivated. For example, if great study music keeps you focused, then stop studying in silence.

The big motivation myth

There's a big myth about motivation that a lot of students believe; I used to think this too. The myth is: *you need to feel motivated before you can study. You shouldn't study if you don't feel like it.* Do you ever feel like this? I used to, until I realized that if you sit around and wait for studying motivation to arrive, you'll be waiting a helluva long time! A common excuse for not studying is that you just don't feel like it. You think you should wait to hit the books until you *want* to study.

The problem is, it's unlikely that study motivation will strike when you're lying on your bed in an M&M coma, five episodes deep into *Modern Family*. Rather than getting motivated and then studying, we have to flip the script. Instead, action most often comes *before* motivation. I used to make this mistake, and it crippled my productivity in my first year of university. This is where a lot of students go wrong – so listen up.

I wish I could give you a magic potion that will make you *want* to study – but I can't. If I could, I would have bottled that sorcery up and I'd be a squillionaire right now, sipping Piña Coladas from a coconut on a Caribbean beach.

Until I've invented this elixir you've *got to actually do the work*. The little-known truth is that motivation only shows its beautiful face once you start gaining momentum, and you have to *start* studying to gain momentum. Once you've ticked a task off your to-do list (best feeling ever, right?!) you'll have started the ball rolling… and this momentum will boost your motivation to continue studying.

The Progress Principle

Slow and steady progress is a more certain route to success than rare big leaps. Harvard Business School professor Teresa Amabile and researcher Steven J Kramer conducted a study with 238 people from seven companies working in project teams (Amabile and Kramer, 2007). Over four months, they asked the participants to complete a survey at the end of each work day questioning them on their emotions, work habits, motivations and what they accomplished – totalling 12,000 entries.

The study found that participants had one of their 'best days' if they made progress on a work task and had one of their 'worst days' if they experienced a setback. On days where the participants made progress, they were happier, more positive and more motivated to keep working. The researchers called this the Progress Principle.

If you want to feel more motivated to study, you need to make progress first. This doesn't have to be big leaps with large study tasks, like writing an essay or passing an exam; small wins such as finishing notes on a hard chapter or getting a correct answer to a question count too. To help you step into action and make progress in your studies, I've come up with eight ways you can combat low study motivation.

Accept low motivation is normal

Even the most driven, hard-working students experience low motivation at times. It doesn't matter how much you want your qualification, there will be times when you'd rather sleep/clean the bathroom/do absolutely anything than study. And that's OK! Feeling unmotivated sometimes does not make you lazy or a failure. It doesn't have to mean anything other than, 'I'm a hard-working student who needs a break'.

Accept that this is normal and be kind instead of badmouthing yourself. Read on to discover the strategies you can use to soldier on and study anyway.

Disrupt your pattern

Have you ever sat on the sofa, knowing you need to study, but you just can't move? One way to make it easier to get from sofa to desk is to disrupt your pattern. To break out of an unmotivated funk, you need to change your state. This means that instead of forcing yourself to start studying immediately, just summon the energy to do something different first.

Go outside and get a few minutes of fresh air, dance around for one song, drink a large glass of cold water, or have a shower. One of these small things should be enough to change your state and shake off that lethargy so you can then go to your desk and study.

Start with a quick win

If you find your lack of motivation often leads you to procrastinate, then let me introduce you to the humble 'quick win'. When you don't want to study, an effective remedy is to ease yourself into your study session. Rather than setting to work on a large study task, like writing an essay, break this down and identify the very first, small step you can take, eg setting up your essay document.

This morning I didn't want to write my weekly blog post. Rather than let a lack of motivation win, I picked my quick win and spent five minutes outlining the points I wanted to include – which was *a lot* easier than starting from a blank page.

When you start with a quick win it's not long until you can check it off your to-do list. Do that and you'll feel a lot more motivated to tackle the next study task... and the next.

Eat the frog first

Now this strategy is the opposite of a quick win, so you have to decide which one will work best for you, or it might be that you switch between them depending on what's holding you back from studying.

Self-development expert Brian Tracy developed the 'eat that frog' method. If I told you that at some point today you have to eat a frog, it would make sense to do it first thing to get it out the way so it's not hanging over you

(Tracy, 2001). It's the same with studying. If you have a large, boring or difficult study task that you know you have to do – do it first to get it out of the way.

Everything you'll do afterwards will feel easier and you'll be more motivated to work through the less frog-like tasks. And you never know, the scary task might not have been as unpalatable as you thought!

Make a task smaller

Seeing the task 'write essay' on your to-do list feels pretty daunting and when a task looks overwhelming, we don't feel motivated to start… which leads to good ol' procrastination. Instead, split your larger study tasks into sub-tasks, which will make it feel like you're progressing quicker. As you tick off each task, you'll feel motivated to continue, but also, you'll have more clarity about what to focus on next.

Some possible sub-tasks for writing an essay could be: set up your essay document; break down the question; brainstorm some content ideas; plan your essay sections; draft your introduction, etc.

Find some motivational quotes

You've worked out your one day and everyday motivations, but sometimes a bit of outside wisdom can really give your studying motivation a boost.

Try spending a little bit of time (but not too much!) looking for quotes that inspire and motivate you to learn and study hard. Make a list or some quick posters you can keep near you in your studies.

A motivational saying I love is, 'A quitter never wins and a winner never quits.' It has a chant-like vibe about it, and I see it as a bit of a call to arms. For me, this was a lifesaver during my second year of university, when I decided to double up my modules *and* retake my entire maths A-level at the same time – a ludicrous decision, for sure! Towards the end of the really intense period, I pinned my will to this quote. Seeing it every day made me dig deeper and push past the fatigue to get my studying done.

Reward your hard work

You're a committed student who is working hard towards your dreams, even if sometimes you'd rather your dreams worked for themselves. You're awesome! Therefore, you deserve regular rewards. To keep you motivated, plan a small treat for the end of every study session such as a chocolate bar, episode of your favourite TV show or a hot bath. Decide on your reward before you start studying to boost your focus and help you keep your eyes on the prize.

Celebrate your achievements

Hands up if your heavy workload often means you start working on the next essay as soon as you submit the first one?

It's easy to always look forward in your studying; forward to the next deadline, the next module. But if you only ever look ahead, you'll miss out on seeing how far you've come. Recognizing your progress will keep you motivated to continue, because you'll see that, however slowly, you're making headway in your studies.

One way I recommend tracking your achievements is to spend a minute at the end of each study session noting down what you achieved in the time. Now you may sometimes feel like you didn't achieve anything, but unless you sat there and didn't even open your books, then you did achieve *something*. Jot it down and feel proud that you took another step forward in your academic journey – because it's these small steps that build over time to success.

Another thing I do is to keep a 'happy things' jar. When you're beavering away with your head stuck in a textbook, it can be hard to notice the small, good things that are happening around you. I keep a 'happy things' jar to help me stop and smell the roses sometimes. See the box for how to make one of your own.

Try this – happy things jar

Find an empty glass jar and some sticky notes. Assign a colour of sticky note to a different area of your life. For me, I chose studying, personal, work and business. Keep the jar and notes on your desk, and every time you think of something happy or something you're proud of, write it on a note, fold it up and stick it in the jar. Here are some ideas for the kind of thing it might be helpful to put in your happy jar:

- getting a good grade in an assignment or exam;
- receiving praise or good feedback from a tutor;
- studying on a Sunday even though you really didn't want to;
- raising your hand and answering a question in a tutorial even though you were scared;

- when your manager compliments your work;
- when you stand up for what's right;
- helping a colleague with something that isn't even your job;
- when you support a friend;
- when you work through an issue with your partner or family member;
- when you make progress on a health or fitness goal.

Whenever you're feeling unmotivated or stressed about studying, take the jar and read some of your notes. Seeing actual evidence of your achievements and happier times will boost your positivity and motivate you to keep going.

What to do when you don't feel like studying

We all have days where we don't want to study, and sometimes that feeling lasts all week. You're grumpy, tired and jealous of your friends who aren't studying and who can come home from work and do nothing. But as we've seen, successful students don't wait until they *want* to study. They know it's important to keep pushing the needle by studying a little pretty much every day.

I used to tell myself that if I force myself to study when I don't want to it will be a waste of time because I won't get good work done. Alas, this isn't true! Even if you don't want to study, you can still do great work.

Therefore, when you don't want to study, you have two options. Option 1 – give up, relax, and make no progress towards your study goals. Or, option 2 – suck it up, study, and make progress towards your study goals. You *can* choose option 1 sometimes – if you know you're on track or that you can make up the time tomorrow. But, realistically, too many days choosing option 1 is going to result in you achieving grades you're not happy with.

Instead, I want you to work consistently towards choosing option 2 in your studies. Put in the effort regularly, no matter how small, and you'll reach success. Here's a strategy to help you focus on the small steps over the big leaps.

'No excuse' study tasks

Create a list of your 'no excuse' study tasks to prompt you into studying, even when you don't want to. These are either the quick study tasks that anyone can fit into their day, or they are tasks with a low-cognitive load, which means they don't require a lot of brain power – perfect for those unmotivated, 'meh' days.

I'm going to walk you through some examples, but it will be most effective if you create your own list of tasks, based on your own studying and the regular tasks you have to complete each week.

5–10-minute 'no excuse' study tasks

- Tidy your desk.
- Create a task list for tomorrow with your top priorities.
- Check your schedule for any clashes (and try to resolve them).
- File your latest notes.

20–30-minute 'no excuse' study tasks

- Review your latest notes. Do you understand them, do you need to add anything else to them?
- Test your knowledge with a quiz or some flashcards.
- Look at your next essay question and break it down so you understand it.
- E-mail your tutor if you don't understand the essay question.
- Tidy your digital files and folders.
- Set up your next essay document (with formatting, sections, header/footer, etc).

45–60-minute 'no excuse' study tasks

- Finish taking notes for a section of your textbook.
- Start some online research for your next essay, bookmarking links for later.
- Breakdown your essay question, work out some possible sections and start compiling notes.
- Create some flashcards or a mind map from your subject notes.

Grab a piece of paper, split it into three and create your own lists of 'no excuse' study tasks using my examples as inspiration. Keep this poster in your main studying folder, on your desk or stuck to your wall, then next time you're lacking study motivation, look at the poster, pick a task and get cracking – no excuses!

Once you've completed a task, you might decide to continue studying because you've gained momentum. But even if you don't keep going, you'll have made some progress which, over time, will develop into a powerful, consistent study habit.

Action steps

- Work out your One Day and Everyday studying motivation.
- Find some motivational quotes that inspire you to study.
- Create a Happy Things jar.
- Create your No Excuse study tasks lists.

Part Three
Organization and productivity

07
Organization

Organization is pretty un-sexy, I know. Unless you're one of those magical people who geeks out over folder structures and loves ironing (teach me please!), organization can feel like a boring minefield – but it doesn't have to be.

Being and staying organized at university or college will help you stay on track with your workload and remove those panicky moments of, 'why aren't my notes in order?' or, 'why is my essay not where I saved it?'

I'm not asking you to organize every inch of your life, but set up a few simple systems now and you'll thank yourself (and me!) later.

Physical studying organization

It's important to have a clear, physical space to store your study materials, even if some of them are online. Over the course of your module, you're going to accumulate a lot of materials and notes. I recommend you buy one folder for every module or subject you're taking; a simple A4 ring binder or lever-arch folder is perfect. Then buy some paper/card dividers to separate your folder materials.

Next, thinking about one module at a time, identify the types of study materials you have.

Here are some of the sections you *could* include in your folder. You might not need all of these, and you might want to add others, so look at this list and then apply the general principles to your own situation.

- Module information such as a handbook or introduction guide, learning outcomes, referencing/citation guide, etc.
- Syllabus or course outline with what you'll be learning and when.
- Important dates such as tutorials, exams and essay/project deadlines.
- Assignments or essays including all guidance for your assignments and then space for your final assignments and tutor feedback.

- Notes.
- Handouts and slides from tutorials.
- Revision material, including any provided by your university, and the material you'll create such as mind maps, quizzes, etc.

Once you've picked the relevant sections, write each section on the sticky-out tab of a divider and then slot them into your folder. Or, if you prefer, you could leave the tabs blank and create a contents list for the front of your folder.

The note-taking dilemma

We'll go into more detail later about choosing a note-taking method, but for now you should decide how you want to store them.

Whatever your note-taking style, I suggest filing your notes to keep them safe and in order. If you choose to type your notes, then file them in a sensible, backed-up, digital folder structure and then print copies to go in your physical folder. I say print them, because notes are pointless if you don't use them after you've made them. Once they're printed, they're easier to review, test yourself with and use to create further revision material.

Personally, I hand-write my notes using an A4 refill pad, which means I can neatly tear out the pages and file them straight away. Each week I remove the next section of notes and store them, in order, in the notes section of my folder. Also, I chose to use just one notebook, even when I studied multiple modules. This meant that on each page of notes I had to clearly state the module code in the corner so as not to mix them up.

You may hate this idea and prefer to use one notebook per module. You may also choose to keep your notes in the notebook so as not to destroy it, or because you think it's blasphemy to rip it apart! What's important is that you choose a method that works for you, keeps your notes in order and makes you feel organized.

Implement this simple but powerful system to make you feel fancy and super organized.

Digital studying organization

If you're at the beginning of your studying journey, set up a digital system now so it's easier to stay organized later… even as your files grow. Don't panic, though, if you're partway through your studies without a clear structure in

Figure 7.1 Suggested file structure

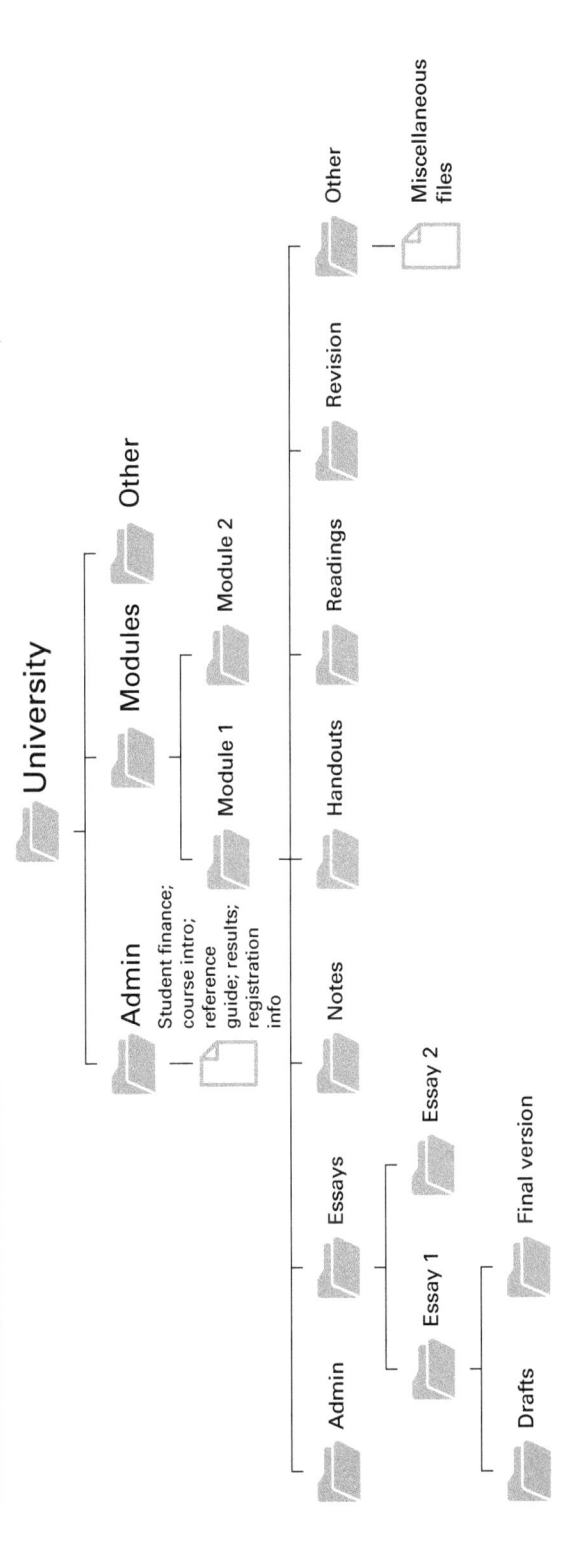

place; it's never too late to get organized, and it shouldn't take too long to find a sensible place for everything.

Here's a suggested file structure that will work as a base for most students. Create any additional folders where necessary.

If you've just started or are about to start studying, then you're good to go. Get into the habit of storing documents correctly as you create or receive them, rather than moving them around later. And if you're partway through your studies, create this structure then spend a little time moving all your files into the correct folders.

File naming

Hands up who's guilty of ever saving documents with vague names such as 'Document 11' or 'Essay 2'? I used to make this mistake and it made organization painful as I wasted time hunting for key documents. You should never have to open a document to know what it is. Your computers have a search function for a reason; if you name a document correctly and misplace it, you should be able to find it by searching for the right key word.

When you're naming your essays or assignments, my top tip is to make sure to include the following: module/class code (so you know which module it's for), essay number or name, and the version number. One of my essays for the Open University was named 'B121_TMA1_V2' which means it was for a module with the code B121, it was essay number 1 (named TMA at the Open University) and it was my second draft so it was version (V) 2. The next draft of the essay would have been 'B121_TMA1_V3' and so on.

If you type your notes, make sure your document titles are clear so that you can understand them. For example, include your module code and, if you're taking notes from a textbook, the chapter your notes are from, eg 'B121_Chapter3_notes' would be for notes from chapter 3 of the course textbook in module B121. If you're taking notes from a variety of sources and readings then you could include the unit or block of work; 'B121_Block1_notes' would be all my notes from block 1 of module B121.

The importance of backups

Lastly, I want to talk to you about an even un-sexier thing – backups. However you decide to take notes and store your materials – backups are **vital**. One Saturday I was coming back from studying at a library and I left my module folder on the bus. This had *all* my handwritten notes from the past few months in it. I was beside myself all evening because, by the time I realized, the bus station was already closed. Very (I-actually-cried-I-was-so-happy) luckily, some beautiful, kind soul handed in my folder and I got it back the next day. Phew!

Imagine the impact if I'd never got my folder back. I had an exam at the end of that module, and without my notes I would have had to start again creating my revision material – this would not only have taken forever, but I probably wouldn't have achieved as good a grade as I did.

Another reason to back up your study material is so you have a safe record of your assignments, feedback and notes to help you later in your studies. A few times now I've started working with a client to help them improve their essay-writing skills, and when I ask them to send me some previously marked essays and their corresponding tutor feedback they can't – either because they deleted it or because they didn't download it from their university website in time. Combine backups with the simple digital file system I've outlined, and you'll always have a record to refer back to in later modules.

Backup methods

There are two main methods of backing up your study materials. You could copy your digital documents to an external hard drive, or you could upload your materials to the cloud using a service like Google Drive, Microsoft OneDrive or DropBox.

Personally, I use DropBox on a paid business plan – but they have a free basic plan for 2GB of storage, which is plenty for all your text-based notes and essay documents. OneDrive looks like a great option if you have a computer with Windows 10, as it's automatically linked – this free plan allows for 5GB. Google Drive is automatically integrated into Android devices, and its free plan has 15GB storage. There are more options out there, and many are free or reasonably priced – choose the one which works for you.

> **Top tip**
>
> I actually back up all my documents twice – first to DropBox, and then to an external hard drive – so I can be even more sure of not losing anything important. I'm now in the habit of backing up my work, but until I was, I set a weekly alarm on my phone to remind me to spend five minutes copying work from my laptop.

Now, you might be thinking, 'That's great Chloe, but I handwrite my notes. How is backing up gonna stop me leaving those on the bus like you did?!' Well, my friend, let me introduce you to the magic of an app called Scannable. I always assumed scanning was only possible on a scanner – but your smartphone's camera can do it too! With a free app like the one I use, simply take a photo of a piece of paper and it will turn it into a scan you can save to your phone as a photo or as a PDF. My favourite, Scannable, is only available for Apple devices, but again, there loads of options out there – for Android, Windows or iOS devices, you could try CamScanner, for example.

If you hand-write your notes, every week spend five minutes scanning every page. You can then file your notes in your physical folder and save the scans to your digital folder *and* either a hard drive or cloud-based service – bingo!

How to prepare yourself and your space

You wouldn't rock up to run a marathon in the wrong clothes, with no sleep, no plan, and on an empty stomach. So, don't sit down to study when you're not ready to do great work, because it's a lot easier to be productive when you're prepared.

There's a French culinary term, *mise en place*, which translates as 'everything in its place', and refers to the setup required before a chef starts cooking. *Mise en place* includes collecting the equipment they'll need, gathering and prepping their ingredients, and getting clear on the plan or recipe they're going to follow. By getting ready, a chef's cooking will go more smoothly, and they'll be able to create a delicious dish quickly so that it's still hot when they serve it. *Mise en place* saves the chef time, and allows them to cook with more focus and without interruptions.

You can apply *mise en place* to your studying too. There are six ways you should set up yourself and your study space to have the most organized and productive study sessions ever, and this process will only take five minutes.

1 Clear your desk

You may have heard the saying, 'tidy space, tidy mind' – well it's true. It's going to be hard to think clearly and study efficiently if your study space is a mess. I am *not* a tidy person (my bedroom doesn't have a floor, it has a floordrobe right now), but my desk is super tidy because I value my productivity.

Before you start studying, spend a few minutes clearing your desk by filing away study materials you don't need right now, taking away plates and cups, and anything else that doesn't belong. Also, try to balance having a lovely study space with necessity. You may need all of those 17 notebooks at some point but right now they're cluttering up your space.

2 Grab everything you'll need

Collect all the study materials and stationery you're going to need for your session, and find any videos or audio clips you'll need too.

3 Remove distractions

Not taking this step is one of the most common mistakes I see students make. For a lot of us, our phones are glued to us all day. This is great for connectivity… but crappy for our studying. It's hard to get stuff done when you're constantly stopping studying 'just for a second' to check your phone.

Now I'm not having a go, because I'm guilty of this too. I know I'm much more productive without my phone next to me, but I struggle to let it go sometimes. Intentional study is hard but necessary. You might spend two hours studying, but you're also responding to phone notifications and Googling non-study stuff. At the end of those two hours you've not achieved all that much, but you also haven't been relaxing. Instead, try your hardest to focus solely on studying when you've decided to study. Then you'll be more productive, complete your study tasks quicker and can relax guilt-free.

Do whatever you need to do to remove your phone as a distraction – put it on silent, set it to do not disturb, turn off notifications or put it out of reach. I put my iPhone on do not disturb, meaning that my family can still call me if there's an emergency, but no other notifications will get through. I then put it on the other side of the room when I want to work.

Turn off the TV or radio, move somewhere as quiet as possible, and close any internet tabs you don't need for studying. There are lots of apps you can get now that block your access to certain sites at times you choose. Cold Turkey (found at getcoldturkey.com) is one option you can download for Windows and Apple computers. Select the websites you want to block and for how long and the app will not let you access them.

4 Grab some study snacks

Make a hot drink and grab a glass of water so you don't have to get up when you're thirsty. Also, who doesn't love a study snack? I would like to tell you I try and pick something healthy but at the moment eating chocolate every day is good for my soul so I'm doing that instead! Grab your favourite snack to give you the brain power for your super studying.

5 Make yourself comfortable

Preparing yourself means removing any chance of your brain making excuses to stop studying. Wear comfortable clothes, grab a lamp if necessary, get a cushion for your chair and take a bathroom break before you start studying. These all sound simple, but it's a good routine to get into, and will boost your productivity for sure.

6 Find the perfect soundtrack

This one is personal preference – I love, love, *love* listening to music while I study. It has to be instrumental music without lyrics, though, as hearing words in my earbuds while I'm trying to read or write words makes my brain go squiggly. And apparently, I'm not the only one. A study from 2012 published in *Work* magazine investigated the effects of background music on performance in a work environment. The researchers played music with and without lyrics and observed the effects on the participants' productivity and attention, ultimately finding that music with lyrics is likely to reduce attention and performance (Shih et al, 2012). Therefore, for focus, music without lyrics should be chosen.

Of course, not everyone will like listening to music while they're trying to concentrate, but there is some research behind the idea. To summarize, it is thought our brains have two attention systems (Vossel et al, 2013). The unconscious system is simple, operates faster and is linked to processing emotions rather than reasoning, while the conscious system allows us to direct our attention to what we want to focus on. Your conscious attention system is what you use to focus on reading your textbook, and your unconscious attention system is scanning the environment for anything important. This would have been useful millions of years ago to make sure a lion didn't creep up on us, but it's not as useful when we're trying to study at home and the hum of the fridge/ticking clock/noisy neighbours is distracting us.

Studying is hard (and sometimes boring), which means we have to work harder to keep our conscious brain focused. But this makes the unconscious part more powerful and more easily distracted. Study music can then be used as a tool to combat this problem. Music (without lyrics, remember) can provide background noise that isn't invasive, makes us feel happier, and can help subdue the unconscious attention system's capacity for distraction.

I would recommend trialling studying in silence and listening to non-lyrical music during different types of study activity. For reading, note taking and essay writing, listening to instrumental music should help you stay focused and engaged on your task. But for revision activities such as testing your knowledge and completing practice exam papers, there are arguments for trying out studying in silence – after all, you will have to sit your actual exam in silence. You should always practice answering questions in exam conditions, ie to the time limit and with your allowed materials, so conducting some study in silence is worthwhile.

There are lots of different types of instrumental music so make sure you try a few before you dismiss it as not working for you. My favourites are either electronica-type music or film and video game soundtracks, but you can also find white noise soundtracks or nature sounds. I have a great hour-long track of a thunderstorm in a rainforest.

Here's a list of some of my favourite soundtracks:

- every *Harry Potter* and *Game of Thrones* soundtrack;
- *The Handmaid's Tale* by Adam Taylor;
- *The Imitation Game* by Alexandre Desplat;
- *Inception* by Hans Zimmer;
- *Jane Eyre* by Dario Marinelli;
- *Taboo* by Max Richter;
- *The Theory of Everything* by Jóhann Jóhannsson;
- *Assassins Creed Revelations* by Jesper Kyd and Lorne Balfe.

And my favourite instrumental artists are:

- Emancipator;
- August Wilhelmsson;
- Audiomachine;
- Two Steps from Hell;
- Kodomo.

There is no right or wrong way of studying, because what matters is what works for *you*. Trial different methods for different studying activities until you've found your successful formula.

How to create an awesome study plan

If you're driving somewhere you've never been before, you'll need a map or a SatNav. Yes, you might be able to find your way there by sheer luck, trying every route or by stopping every few minutes to ask for directions – but it will take forever, you'll spend more on fuel, and you'll arrive tired and hungry. Well, the same goes for studying – you'll struggle to reach a new study goal without a study plan.

There are six key benefits of creating a study plan:

- You'll know what you need to do and when – no guesswork required.
- You'll save time having one master study plan rather than working from lots of individual plans on scraps of paper.
- You'll know quickly if you fall behind or take the wrong direction so that you can course correct.
- You'll be able to prioritize your important study tasks so you don't waste time being busy on unimportant or less important study tasks.
- And, ultimately, you'll achieve your study goals and achieve the grades you really, really want.

Here are three steps you can follow to create an effective study plan.

1 Get to know your course

Read *all* your course or module guidance material such as the module guide or handbook. Try to find out the structure of your course and how it will be delivered, eg face-to-face or online tutorials, the frequency of tutorials and assessments, etc. Then find out *how* you will be assessed. How many exams, essays, group projects and so on will you have? Locate a syllabus to discover what you'll be learning and whether you have any learning aims or outcomes.

2 Track the important dates

It is your responsibility to know and remember all key dates for tutorials, office hours, group projects, presentations, essays, practice tests, revision sessions, exams, etc. The way to do this (without feeling constantly overwhelmed) is to record these dates in the best way for you. I recommend tracking important dates twice.

First, record these with the same method you use for organizing your non-study life, whether that's a physical diary or planner, digital calendar app or wall planner. Then, create lists of each type of date and file these in the front of your folder – for example, a list of tutorial dates and a list of essay due dates. This will give you a clear, at-a-glance overview of all your upcoming commitments, and you'll be able to see your progress and boost your motivation by ticking or highlighting each date you meet.

3 Create a week-by-week study plan

Some of you may be lucky and find that your university or college creates a weekly plan for you. For example, the Open University had an online tool displaying the expected reading each week along with any tutorial, essay or exam dates. This was so helpful – I could tell immediately whether I was on track, ahead or behind.

If your university doesn't provide this plan, then you need to create one. And even if it does, like the Open University, you might want to create your own so that you can add your own deadlines, such as when you're going to plan your essays and when you're going to start your revision.

Using all the information you found in step two (lists of dates, the syllabus, etc), map out the study tasks you have to complete each week. It may help to start by plugging in your due dates and then you can work backwards to identify what needs completing by when.

Let's say you have an essay due in four weeks' time. Your master plan may look like Table 7.1 for the next four weeks.

You start by putting in the due date of your essay, 26 November, and decide you want one week to write the essay and a few days to plan it. Looking at the topic of that essay you'll need to read three chapters of one of your textbooks to be able to answer it well. Given that today is 1 November, that means you have just over two and a half weeks to read and take notes on those three chapters. You may add in other tasks, such as e-mailing your tutor with any questions once you've planned your essay, or breaking down the essay question earlier on so you can keep it in mind as you read and take notes on the relevant material.

You can choose how you format this plan; a table like this often works well, so you could create it as a spreadsheet in Microsoft Excel or as a

Table 7.1 Essay study plan

Week	Study tasks
Week 1 1 November	• Breakdown/understand question for strategy essay • Read Chapter 1 • Read Chapter 2
Week 2 8 November	• Finish reading Chapter 2 • Read Chapter 3
Week 3 15 November	• Finish reading Chapter 3 • Plan essay • E-mail tutor with any questions on the essay • Write essay
Week 4 22 November	• Write essay • Strategy essay due 26 November

document in Microsoft Word – or using similar software. You might also want to colour-code the tasks by type such as due dates, essay-related tasks, reading, tutorials, etc.

Make sure you back up your master plan and make it accessible to you by printing it and sticking it in your folders, and turning it into a PDF or image you can view on your device wherever you are.

This task is probably going to take you a little while, but I promise you it will be worth it. In the next chapter, we'll look at how to use your master plan to keep you on track.

How to actually stick to your study plan

The real work starts now, because the plan will only work for you, and get you higher grades, if you stick to it. You don't have to be perfect – because no one is – but you do have to keep trying. Here are five ways you can stick to your master study plan.

1 Remember your reasons for studying

When you're struggling to get motivated, look back at why you're doing this. Find your 'one day' and 'everyday' motivation lists (see Chapter 6) and have another read to reconnect with your big reasons for studying and what day-to-day things motivate you to study.

2 Remember your study goals

Your goals aren't going to meet themselves – so think about what you want to achieve, to motivate you to stick to your plan. Visualize how kickbutt you'll feel when you've met your goals. If you're currently achieving 50 per cent essay scores and you want to achieve 70 per cent, think about what meeting this goal will do for you. You'll have learned new study skills that will help you achieve higher essay grades in all future studying, relieving the pressure and making you feel more confident every time you hit the submit button. You'll also achieve a higher degree classification, which could open up more career and life opportunities for you.

3 Stock up on accountability

Your studying success is down to you and pretty much you alone. However, when you are accountable to only yourself, you can choose to screw yourself over by ditching your plan. Therefore, consider expanding your accountability by telling friends, family and colleagues you care about what your study goals are and when you're going to study. Ask them to check in on you to make sure you're doing what you said you would. You don't want to have to tell your loved ones you didn't want to do the work, so having people in your corner to pooh-pooh your excuses, cheer you on or kick you up the butt will inspire you to do the work you know you should do.

4 Be flexible

Flexibility is key to making sure your studying gets done, even when life happens. Enrolling in a qualification is a big commitment, and you might need to be flexible at times to prioritize your studying in the way it deserves.

If you've fallen behind or are struggling to fit your education into your life, could you get up earlier or go to bed later depending on your energy levels? If you're more productive in the mornings, can you rearrange your commute, or your wake-up and bed times, to allow you some early study time?

What can you do to save time in your week? Could you order your food shopping online? Could you change up your exercise routine to achieve the same benefit in less time? Could you meal prep at the weekends to save time cooking each evening?

Everyone's studying situation is different, so maybe these suggestions don't work for you. But it's your responsibility to think up ways you *can* flex your schedule to make enough hours for your studies.

5 Create a back-up plan

Sometimes your schedule will start to fill up, and it will seem easier to just ditch the studying and try to catch up next week. Maybe this is necessary sometimes, say if a family member is ill, or there's an emergency at work, but for less serious obstacles you should still try to stick to your plan.

NYU Psychology professor Peter Gollwitzer conducts research on goals and plans. A goal intention (Gollwitzer, 1993) looks like this – 'I intend to pursue X'. For example, I intend to study for eight hours on Saturday. Setting a goal intention increases the likelihood of reaching it, but there's a problem – obstacles.

Gollwitzer (1999) explains that obstacles often hinder us from turning our goals into actions. Things get in the way that stop us sticking to our study plans. As well as creating a goal intention you should also create a back-up plan, or 'implementation intention', that identifies the action you will take if you hit a bump in the road – 'If situation Y arises, I will perform response Z'.

For our studying on a Saturday example, one obstacle could be that your sister and her children are thinking of visiting this weekend, which could scupper your studying plans. To help you achieve this goal, use Gollwitzer's implementation intention to create a back-up plan. For example, 'If my family comes to visit, I will get up early on Saturday and Sunday to study before we start any activities.' Or, 'If my family comes to visit, I will study on Sunday evening once they leave and rearrange my Monday cinema trip to the week after.'

Look at your study plan each week and think of an obstacle that could stand in your way of completing your tasks. Then think about what you can do to overcome this obstacle and write this down as an 'If Y… then Z…' statement. Gollwitzer (1999) explains that implementation intentions aid goal achievement by passing control from your own conscious, which could decide to ditch the goal, to the action that you've already decided.

Work–life balance

There are a lot of differing opinions on what work–life balance means and how to achieve it, so I want to give you my view from a student who returned to study as a mature, distance *and* workplace learner, and from my experience in teaching similar students how to achieve higher grades.

I truly believe we can do and have everything we want in life. We can have a fulfilling career, be a successful student, have a tidy, beautiful home, have a high level of fitness, have an exciting social life, and be a great friend, parent, child, sibling, etc.

But we can't have it all at once. Studying alongside a busy life is like performing that circus act with the spinning plates on sticks. Each plate represents an area of your life such as studying, work, family, health, etc. The more plates you have, the harder you have to work to keep them spinning.

We rush around, busy, busy, busy, spinning each plate before moving on to the next one, doing all we can to stop them dropping. We're studying hard, then making room for family time, then squeezing in cooking healthy meals, going for a run, seeing friends so they don't forget who we are, cleaning the bathroom, washing laundry because we keep running out of clean pants…

After a while we're exhausted. We can't push ourselves any harder, so a few plates start to drop. We feel ashamed that we can't handle everything, that we're just not good enough because we look around us and on social media and we see others seemingly doing it all.

The solution *isn't* for you to push harder. Instead, the solution is to remove some of the plates and put them to the side for a while so that you can keep up. If you reduce the number of plates you're trying to spin, then you'll be able to keep them all spinning well… and you'll be *a lot* happier.

I think it's damaging to talk about work–life balance because it implies that balance is possible, that there's some art form to spinning a shedload of plates without killing yourself and that your problem is that you just haven't learned it yet.

Therefore, rather than work–life balance, I see work, life, studying (and everything else) as seasonal instead. There will be seasons of your life when studying is your priority, which means you have to decide which of your other plates you can stop trying to spin for a while.

For me, when I've been in a season of essay after essay, I have to accept that my house isn't going to be as clean as I want it to be and that my ideal, non-studying fitness routine isn't possible right now. For you, it might be your social life or hobbies that have to take a back seat.

I fought hard against this idea for so long and at times I still do. I hate living in an untidy house, and I feel shame when I go to my friends' houses and they're spotless. But it's taken me time to realize we all have a different set of plates and they all mean different things to us. My beautiful, antique, willow-patterned plate – that I must keep spinning – is seeing my friends, because they keep me grounded as well as lift me up. Your precious, non-negotiable plate might be your family or your health or having a beautiful home.

Once your studying calms down for a while, whether it's in a week, a few weeks or a few months, you can add some of your other plates back in.

We have to stop judging ourselves on our plate-spinning abilities and instead accept that we can't do everything at once. We're struggling not because we're not working hard enough, but because it's *not possible to do everything at once*. If we remove this have-it-all version of work–life balance as a goal, then we remove this unobtainable burden and give ourselves permission to thrive.

If you're in a season of studying right now and you feel overwhelmed and unhappy, have a look at the plates you're spinning and decide which you can put to the side for a while. If that feels hard, remember that it won't be forever. That's the beauty of seasons, they don't stay the same forever.

Action steps

- Set up/edit your physical folders, digital filing system, and back-up routine.
- Test studying with different types of non-lyrical music, and silence.
- Record your important dates (twice).
- Create your master study plan.
- Look at your next week of studying and create implementation intentions to help you stick to your study plan.

08
Productivity

Have you ever spent the day organizing your sock drawer, cleaning the bathroom, being busy, busy, busy… but not starting your essay like you said you would? Have you ever had days where you tick a zillion things off your to-do list without getting that *one* important study task completed?

If you answered yes, then you have fallen into the busy trap – believing you're being productive, when really, you're being busy. Being *busy* means working or studying a lot. Being *productive* means working on the important study tasks that will move you closer to your goals. As personal development and leadership expert Robin Sharma (2014) once tweeted: 'Don't confuse activity with productivity. Many people are simply busy being busy.'

For busy students, their days run them. They study for hours each week, but they still feel behind, and their grades aren't getting any higher. Whereas productive students own their day, and maximize their time, so they can tick off the *right* study tasks and make progress towards their study goals.

Everyone falls into the busy trap at times, including me, so I'm not going to dish out a slap on the wrist for any 'busy' students out there. Instead, successful students notice when they're slipping into busy-ness and take action to move towards productivity instead.

Best study self

Achieving a degree, or similar qualification, requires a long chain of individual decisions to study even when you'd rather be doing something else. This takes self-discipline – a key study skill all students must develop in order to be successful.

The first step to becoming more self-disciplined is to increase your awareness of how *you* study best. We're all different, with various strengths, weaknesses, desires and situations. Ask yourself: What do you need to be a productive and effective student? What do you need to be the best student you can be?

Here are five questions to help you work out your best study self.

1 What time of day are you the most productive?

Are you an early bird who's most effective in the morning? Or do you do your best work in the evening as a night owl?

2 Where do you get your best studying done?

Focus on the 'best' part here. You may like studying in bed or on the sofa but think about your most productive, kick-butt study sessions – where do they happen? Is it at your desk, the kitchen table, a local café or library?

Do you like to study in the same place or are you more productive when you mix it up? I am my best study self when I work at my desk, but I also like going to cafés sometimes – though I always end up ordering *way* too much food!

3 Do you prefer shorter or longer study sessions?

Are you good at fitting in quick, 30-minute study sessions throughout your day, or does it take you longer to get into your groove? Have a think about the ideal length of your study sessions.

4 What background noise makes you the most productive?

Do you swear by studying in silence, or with some kind of music? If it's music, what works for you? Is it white noise, nature sounds, music with lyrics or music without lyrics?

Again, try to keep in mind that this is about your best study self, not just about what you enjoy the most. One of my favourite ways to de-stress is to sing at the top of my lungs to my favourite music, but I know I don't study effectively with lyrics, so it's instrumental music without lyrics that works for me.

5 What do you need for a great study session?

And lastly, what do you need around you to be your best study self? Do you need great tea, coffee or snacks? Do you need a tidy study space, or fresh flowers and a candle on your desk?

Think about the little study extras that always boost your productivity and motivation.

Try this – my best study self

Once you have your answers, turn this list into a mind map poster. In the middle of a plain piece of paper write 'my best study self'. Then around the outside, add all of your answers, so you create one list of all the things you need to be a great student.

Here's my list.

Figure 8.1 My best study self

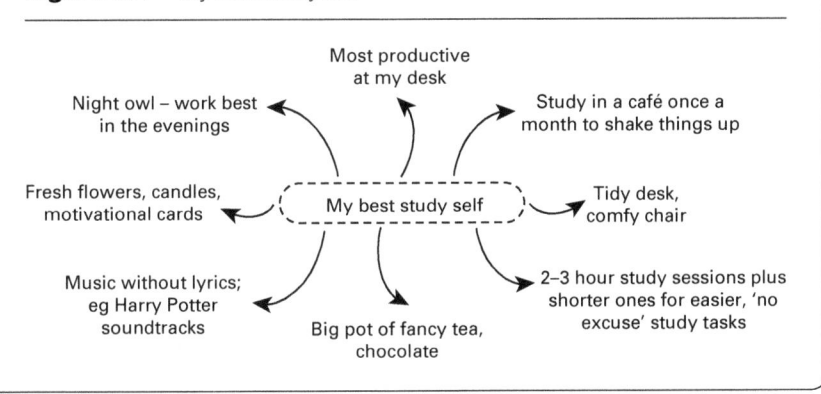

My best study self
- Most productive at my desk
- Night owl – work best in the evenings
- Study in a café once a month to shake things up
- Fresh flowers, candles, motivational cards
- Tidy desk, comfy chair
- Music without lyrics; eg Harry Potter soundtracks
- Big pot of fancy tea, chocolate
- 2–3 hour study sessions plus shorter ones for easier, 'no excuse' study tasks

Now you've worked out how you study best, work *with* these preferences rather than against them. For years I've wanted to be a morning person even though I'm a night owl. I tried to fight this, but I finally realized it was a waste of my time, energy and happiness and that I should work with my strengths instead. I scheduled all my weekday study sessions for the evening to increase the chance that I could stick to them, improving my self-discipline.

How to plan for a productive week

In the last chapter, you created your master study plan identifying your weekly reading, activities and assessments. Now it's time to take this further and set yourself up for the most productive study week ever. Planning perhaps isn't the most exciting thing to do, but if you want to get to the end of each study week having ticked off your entire to-do list, then a little planning needs to happen. Try to find 10 to 15 minutes each weekend to go through the following tasks.

1 Check you're on track

Use your master plan to see if you're on track, ahead or behind schedule. If you're behind, come up with a plan to catch up, whether that's arranging more study sessions, prioritizing your workload or rearranging your personal plans.

2 Work out your tasks and priorities

A lot of students write down absolutely everything they need to do and call this their to-do list. They focus on working through each task, but for every task they check off, they seem to add two to the bottom. Instead, work out what your priorities are, then schedule your study time to make it happen.

Look at the study tasks listed for the next week in your master study plan and think about your current study goals (eg to increase your essay grade by 5 per cent). Use your plan and goals to work out your priority study tasks. Which tasks will help you move towards your goals and the grades you want? Priority study tasks for improving your essay grade could be: review tutor feedback from your last essay; break down the next essay question; or learn how to reference correctly (maybe you lost marks for this last time). Write these down and label them as priorities.

Next, identify the other study tasks you want to complete and add these to your list. These are the nice-to-have tasks. For example: watch lecture video; type up notes; or complete additional reading. The focus of your study sessions should always be on completing your priority tasks first. Once all these tasks are completed, you can move onto your nice-to-have tasks. This way, if something comes up which prevents you getting all your study sessions in, the important work will already be done, and you'll have made progress towards your study goals.

3 Identify your commitments

Identify all your time obligations for the week. Take into account work, commuting, the school run, appointments, events, etc, so you can work out when you have time for studying.

4 Schedule your study sessions

Looking at your task list you should be able to estimate how many hours you should study this week. Then physically add these study sessions to your planner or calendar. It's really important that you don't leave studying to chance because, if you plan out your study sessions, there's a lot more chance of them actually happening. Entrepreneur Chris Ducker advises, 'If it doesn't get scheduled it doesn't get done' (Ducker, 2017).

If you don't have enough time for studying, what can you do about it? Either you have to suck it up and study more next week (not an option you can choose that often), or you have to flex your schedule by delaying, changing or deleting some items to create more study time. Are there any events or appointments you can move around or change slightly so they're shorter or closer to home? Could you take a day off work or ask to work from home to save commuting time?

Only you know your schedule and how important or urgent each commitment is, but there will always be *something* you can do to free some time for studying.

Study session planner

Once you've planned your week and scheduled your study sessions, the next step is to *do the studying*. To help you take the plunge, Figure 8.2 shows my favourite tool for super-productive study sessions. You can download a template for this from my website (chloeburroughs.com) or koganpage.com/return-to-study-handbook.

I created this planner to incorporate everything I've talked about to boost your organization and productivity, ie rewards, priority tasks, achievements, preparing for success, etc.

This printable planner has 12 sections to complete as you study to guarantee a wildly productive study session.

First, you'll add the date and then go through the six-step 'prepare for success' process I walked you through in Chapter 7. Check these off as you get ready to study. Next there's a space for your task list, separated into priority and nice-to-have study tasks. Then there's a Pomodoro tracker and procrastination list, which we'll come to shortly. There's also space to track your hydration, identify your post-study treat and then, once you've finished studying, track all your achievements and progress you've made.

Figure 8.2 Study session planner

STUDY SESSION PLANNER

Date

Hydration *(glasses)*

Pre-study checklist
- Clear desk
- Everything you need
- Remove distractions
- Snacks and drink
- Comfort
- Soundtrack

Post-study treat

Achievements

Priority tasks *(do these first)*

Next steps

Nice-to-have tasks *(do these next)*

Reflections

Pomodoro ratio	Completed

Notes

Procrastination list

It can also be helpful to spend a minute reflecting on your study session; I've given you a few lines to note down anything you notice that made you more or less productive. For example, maybe you stuck to working on your priority tasks first, meaning you finished studying being proud of your achievements. Or, maybe you struggled to stay focused… and you noticed it was because you had your phone next to you. Reflection can help you work out what you could do differently next time (ie put your phone out of reach) to improve your studying just a little bit.

Lastly, write down your next steps and the tasks you want to complete in your next study session, and use the notes section to record any random studying thoughts such as reminders to e-mail your tutor or an idea for your upcoming essay.

Test out this method and see if it works for you. You might want to take your favourite aspects and create your own template because you'll experience the most productivity when you take ownership of your study strategies.

Study breaks

When you've got a task list as long as your arm, and not enough hours in the day, the idea of taking breaks from studying seems laughable. But working solidly for hours at a time, and *not* taking any breaks, is actually counterproductive, because it dramatically reduces cognitive ability and focus. As you study, your brainpower starts to fade... but it's not all bad news, because taking small, frequent breaks refreshes your brain and your productivity so you can keep going.

At the University of Illinois, psychology professor Alejandro Lleras and postdoctoral fellow Atsunori Ariga conducted a study on productivity and attention (Lleras and Ariga, 2011). The researchers asked 84 participants to work on a repetitive computer task for 50 minutes.

The participants were split into four equal groups. The 'control' group were asked to work on the task for the full time of 50 minutes without stopping. The other three groups were told four numbers at the beginning of the task and told that they might show up on the screen during the task. The 'digit-ignored' group were asked to ignore the numbers if they appeared and continue working. The 'switch' group were asked to stop and inform the researchers if one of the four numbers appeared on their screen. The 'no-switch' group were also told to stop and tell the researchers but then they weren't actually shown the numbers. That means that out of the four groups, three of them worked on the task continuously for the 50 minutes, and only one group ('switch') took two short breaks to respond to the numbers that appeared on their screens.

The researchers discovered that the performance of the participants in the 'control', 'no-switch' and 'digit-ignored' groups declined over the 50 minutes, but the performance in the 'switch' group remained constant. Their brief mental breaks allowed them to stay focused for longer. Lleras proposes that 'deactivating and reactivating your goals allows you to stay focused'. And that 'when faced with long tasks… it's best to impose short breaks on yourself' so you can stay focused for longer.

So even if you feel you should glue your butt to your chair for hours because you have a shedload of studying to do, take short breaks often to stay focused and productive for hours.

The Pomodoro Technique

Successful students work really hard, yes… but they also work really smart. Let me introduce you to the seriously smart, yay-to-study-breaks, productivity hack called the Pomodoro Technique. This is a time-management tool created in the 1980s by Italian university student France Cirillo, now a business consultant. He trialled studying in intervals of 25 minutes to see if it would boost his productivity, and he timed himself using a kitchen timer shaped like a tomato, or pomodoro (Cirillo, 2019).

This technique sounds really simple but to reap the benefits you must study with *absolute focus* for those 25 minutes – no distractions, no interruptions, no 'just one scroll' on Instagram or Facebook. Use the Pomodoro Technique correctly, and you'll take control of your time and study sessions rather than feeling like time is running away from you. You'll eliminate fatigue, so you can study productively for longer, and you'll learn how to control procrastination by training yourself not to give in to distractions. This technique will even boost your motivation – you'll develop the habit of studying even when you don't want to, so you'll make progress, gain momentum and be more eager to keep studying.

Here are the five simple steps of the Pomodoro Technique:

1 Decide on one study task to focus on first – no multitasking allowed.

2 Set a timer for 25 minutes and study without interruptions on your task.

3 Once the timer sounds, add a tally mark on a piece of paper to signify one completed Pomodoro.

4 Take a five-minute break to move around, stretch or grab a quick snack.

5 Once your five minutes is up, repeat these intervals until you've completed four Pomodoros (or less if you run out of study time) and then take a longer 30-minute break.

There are some rules you want to keep in mind, to make sure you get the full benefit of this simple but powerful productivity technique.

1 Taking breaks is non-negotiable

Sometimes the Pomodoro will drag, but other times you'll get into the flow and won't want to stop when the timer goes off. It's still important to take a break to refresh your brain so you can come back and do great work for longer. Finish your sentence, then use your five minutes to move around – resist the temptation to power through. (I like to have a solo dance party for one song during my break!)

2 Keep a procrastination list

When you're studying, random thoughts and tasks will pop into your head such as 'text Mum back' or 'look up cinema times for tomorrow'. Your brain would rather do anything than study, so it tries to give you something more exciting and easier to do than read or write an essay. But successful, disciplined students don't respond to distractions.

You don't want to stop studying to do the task, but you also don't want to forget about it; instead, use a procrastination list. Keep a piece of paper or sticky note (not your phone!) next to you as you study with the Pomodoro Technique. Whenever a random thought or task pops into your brain, stop for five seconds, note it down then get straight back to work. Once your study interval is over you can tackle the tasks on the list.

Using a procrastination list gets over the potential obstacle of the Pomodoro Technique, and trains your brain over time to not act on every impulse and thought. The more you use this technique, the easier you'll find it to be productive as a default.

3 Switch up the study/break ratio

The traditional ratio of 25/5 is a great one to start with, and works for study tasks such as note taking or revising, where you're trying to process a lot of information at once. But feel free to experiment with different timings to find what works for you.

If you find the timer always goes off when you're in flow, then try studying for 45 minutes and then taking a 10-minute break. When I'm writing an essay (or this book!) I use this 45/10 method; I find that for this kind of task, it takes longer to organize my thoughts and get into the flow.

The dangers of multitasking

One common obstacle to productive studying is multitasking – performing two tasks at the same time. Multitasking is often celebrated as a desirable skill or a trait to boast about. Job descriptions list 'the ability to juggle multiple tasks at once' as an essential skill, and women in particular tend to be praised for being good multitaskers. We've learned to pride ourselves on our multitasking abilities, believing it makes us more productive and effective.

But the truth is that there's no such thing as multitasking, at least not in the sense that most of us use it. There are only two instances where multitasking *is* possible. Firstly, multitasking is possible if one or both of the tasks are automatic and don't require thinking, for example, eating dinner while watching TV. And secondly, it's possible if the tasks use different brain processes and have a low cognitive load, meaning they use less brain power. For example, a person can iron their clothes and follow along with the storyline of a TV programme.

Therefore, the type of multitasking that doesn't work is trying to do two study tasks at once or trying to do almost any task in combination with studying. Studying while listening to non-lyrical background music is fine, as is studying while eating or drinking.

But studying while watching TV, listening to a podcast, talking to your friend/partner, replying to messages, scrolling through Instagram… these are all a big no-no. When we're multitasking, we think we're getting more done – but switching between tasks, or stopping studying every few minutes to do something else, is seriously unproductive. Multitasking doesn't actually mean doing two things at the same time. Instead, it means switching quickly between two tasks over and over (and probably doing them both less well).

Author Guy Winch (2014) explains that our brains only have a finite amount of attention and productivity, meaning that when we try to multitask, we are wasting energy. When you switch between two or more tasks, it takes time for your brain to reacquaint itself with each task and that time is lost forever. Also, if you're task-switching it takes longer to get 'in the zone', which further wastes time and productivity. In fact, Meyer and Kieras (1997) explain that even though each switch may only waste a few tenths of a second, if you add up all the switches in a day, you could easily be wasting *40 per cent* of your productive time.

Let's say you're working on an essay and you notice an e-mail come in from your tutor. You open the e-mail and read that your tutorial next week is moving to a different day so you check your calendar to make sure you can make it before going back to working on your essay.

You've just switched contexts. This might not seem like a big deal because it only took two minutes, but it will take time for your brain to get back into the flow of essay writing. You might try to finish off your sentence and realize you can't, so you read back a bit to try to remember what this section was about. You might have even lost your train of thought completely, so you waste time trying to remember what you were going to say next. This lost time could have been prevented if you had closed your e-mails down and removed the temptation to switch contexts.

Even if you believe you're a good multitasker, I highly recommend that you try to focus on single-tasking in your studying, to improve your productivity and save time.

> **Tip – tricks to stop multitasking**
>
> Here are two simple things you can try to stop multitasking:
>
> - **Remove distractions before you start**. We talked about this in the last chapter but closing down your e-mails, moving your phone and turning off the TV will all help you resist the urge to multitask.
> - **Use the Pomodoro Technique** to compel you to *just* study. The ticking timer should remind you that studying is your sole focus.

How to study effectively when you have a job

After a long day at work, the last thing you want to do is study all evening. You're tired and just want to faceplant the sofa... but you know you need to study in order to keep up with your workload and not have to pull all-nighters. On your commute home you tell yourself you *will* study tonight. But when you open the front door, all your other responsibilities step up and flick you on the forehead – the house is a mess, dinner's not cooked, your partner or kids want attention.

I know what it's like to work a long day then have to study when you get home. I did this for over four years with my degree, then a year with my creative writing qualification, then another year starting this business – all on top of working full-time. I know what it's like to feel tired but have so much to do that you can't give in and just go to bed. To throw your good intentions out the window, ditch the books, tell yourself you'll study tomorrow… and then be faced with an even scarier reality the next day when you look at your task list.

It's hard to study after work, I get it, but it's a necessary evil to bag the good grades. In Chapter 2 I shared lots of tips for how to study effectively as a workplace learner alongside your job. But I want to give you a few more simple strategies for how to find the time, energy and motivation to study after work.

Know when you're going to study

Sometimes it feels like you come home, eat, then have to go straight to bed. Our evenings don't feel long, but there *will* be snippets of time for everyone where you can fit in some study. Author Jessica Turner describes 'fringe hours' as the pockets of time we already have in our day – such as first thing before your kids wake up, in the office before you start work, during your lunch break, during naptime, as soon as you get home, after your kids are asleep, etc (Turner, 2015).

Fringe hours have a cumulative power. Short bursts of studying often don't feel valuable or useful, but just 30 minutes of planned, intentional studying most days adds up to real, tangible progress. So, have a look at where your fringe hours are in your day and evening, and choose which ones you're going to use to study.

Identify your key task

A guaranteed way to waste time is to sit down at your desk after work without a clear study plan. I've caught (and still catch) myself doing this at times; I've come home from work, opened my books, checked my e-mails quickly, flicked through my notes… I try to start studying but, without focus, the only thing I achieve is hours sat in the chair.

To make the most of your precious after-work study time, always work out your study tasks before you start. The night before, or maybe just before you leave work to come home, look at your master study plan and then write your one, two or three priority study tasks onto a sticky note so you have no excuse not to dive straight in.

Don't give yourself a chance to faff about

Do you ever get home and make that big mistake where you sit down on the sofa for 'just a minute' and suddenly you're paralysed and can't bring yourself to move to your desk? I am very good at procrastinating and stalling when I get home, so to make sure studying actually happens, I've created a no-faffing study routine – consider doing the same. Here's mine: as soon as I get home, I take my shoes off and switch the kettle on. I go upstairs, get changed and open my laptop and books. I go straight downstairs, make a pot of tea then come back upstairs and start studying. No faffing, no phone, no 'I'll just sit down for a minute and quickly check Facebook'.

Make use of the momentum of coming home by creating a no-faff study routine that works for you.

Study during your commute

Another way to maximize your studying time is to study during your commute to and from work. The study tasks you can complete depend, obviously, on your type of commute – whether it's walking, driving or taking public transport. There are two caveats here. Firstly, it shouldn't need to be said but do not place studying above safety! If you drive to work and are likely to get distracted, choose a less taxing task for your commute, or a different time of day to study. Secondly, if you would rather study at another time so you can relax during your commute – then do that. For example, sometimes my favourite way of spending my commute is to host a solo, very loud concert in my car. Singing my heart out de-stresses me and allows me to come home and study in the evening with more energy.

Walking, driving or public transport

- Listen to motivational podcasts that inspire you to learn and be a better student.
- Learn through subject-specific podcasts or audiobooks. Find some audio material related to your course and broaden your learning.
- Listen to any study materials included in your course.

- Record yourself speaking your notes and play it back during your commute.
- Create a test-yourself audio file if you walk to and from work. Create some flashcards using your study material then record yourself reading the question, pausing for 10 to 20 seconds, and then reading the answer. When you're walking, play the audio through your headphone and in that pause, try to answer the question correctly

Public transport only

While you can also listen to motivational podcasts, knowledge-broadening audiobooks, course-related audio material or your own recorded notes on public transport, you can complete a much larger range of study tasks when your attention is greater.

- Note taking from a textbook – if it's not too bumpy.
- Skim reading and adding notes into a textbook's margins for note taking later.
- Planning your week and scheduling your study sessions.
- Testing yourself with flashcards.
- E-mailing your tutor.
- Brainstorming ideas for your next essay.

How to study with a family

Now I don't have children, so I can't give first-hand advice here. But I do have a lot of friends, clients and members of my audience who study alongside raising a family and I've asked them for their best advice.

Some of the strategies are the same as studying alongside a job, so you want to plan your week, lean on your support network, plan rewards, and study with intention. But here are some family-specific study strategies – see if any of them will work for you.

Get them on board

I receive e-mails often from students whose kids or partner or parents don't respect their study time or boundaries. It's hard for anyone, child or adult, to have less of you than they're used to, and studying might in some ways be compared to having another child who needs *a lot* of your undivided attention.

Talk to your children, and anyone else in your close family, about your studying. Ask them for the support you need and remind them that this won't last forever. Explain why you decided to study, what you're enjoying about it and what you are looking forward to doing with your education. Use this as an opportunity to teach them about the value of education, hard work and personal growth.

Get them on board by explaining what opportunities your studying and a qualification will do for you and your career but also for them. Will it mean more money for holidays and treats, or a happier home environment because you'll be able to get a job in a fulfilling, enjoyable field?

Set expectations

When I was completing my degree, I would often come home from work, say hi to my boyfriend quickly and then disappear upstairs telling him I had to study. I'd often get frustrated if he called me down or tried to ask when I'd be finished. I'm ashamed to think of it now but I used to think, and sometimes actually respond angrily with, 'I'll be finished in two years!' or patronisingly, 'I just don't know, OK? I've got lots to do.'

It's easy to get wrapped up in our studying and forget about the other people whose lives are also affected by our education. When I was studying in the evening my boyfriend didn't know when to expect me downstairs. He wouldn't know whether he should wait to make plans, or start a movie, or go out with friends… because I didn't tell him.

Luckily, I learned about the importance of setting expectations for when I would spend time with my friends and family. This is a great tool not just for your children, but also anyone who wants or needs your attention and time. Now, when I get home, I tell my boyfriend three things: the exact study tasks I'll be working on, why they're important, and what time I will be free. This helped focus my attention but also brought him into my studying world and let him know when it was our time.

This could be a great technique for children as well; you're explicitly telling them that you're not free right now, this is what you're doing, and that you will be free at this time to spend time with them.

Ask for help

Could anyone else in your family help out around the house a little more to free up some of your time for studying? Or do you have friends and family who could offer up their babysitting services every so often to help you fit in some uninterrupted study time?

Create family study time

If you have school-aged children, then consider trying to create some slots in your week where you study together. The idea is to spend time with them at the same time as improving their focus on their homework – as they see you working hard too.

These sessions may not be your most focused study time but could be a perfect opportunity to work on those 'no excuse' study tasks that don't require as much brain power, such as filing your notes, planning your week or skim-reading a chapter before note taking.

You can even turn these sessions into a teaching experience by spending a few minutes at the end of your study and homework session talking about what you got up to. You can share your achievements and progress, and encourage them to do the same. You can also bring up any challenges or mistakes you both faced and discuss ways to overcome them next time. This way, you're getting some studying done, they're getting homework done, you're spending time together *and* you're teaching them valuable lessons in work ethic and self-awareness.

Connect with others

All situations in life are easier to get through when you know others are on the same journey. Throughout my studies, I've always had at least one friend who's also studying while working – which has been great for those days when I just want to vent to someone who understands.

Likewise, try to connect with other studying parents to commiserate, celebrate and support each other through your similar situations. If you have local friends who are studying parents, could you even do a babysitting swap once in a while? One week you could look after their child, and the next they take yours, to give you both some uninterrupted study time.

Create time elsewhere

We can create more study time by speeding up our other commitments. I've mentioned this before but meal prepping, online shopping, outfit planning or asking your children to take on more chores can all help to save time you can then spend on studying.

How to create a kick-butt study routine

I wish I could teach just one study routine that will work for every student, studying all subjects, at all times… but that's not possible. You need to create a personalized study routine by testing and tweaking your methods until you've found what works for you.

Studying is a long journey and, like any long journey, course correction will be required to keep you on track. To help you reflect on and fine-tune your study routine I've created a 10-minute process called the Sunday Study Review.

Make it a habit to complete this review every week to look back on your last seven days of studying so you can prepare for the next. Over time, these small changes to your roadmap will bring you closer to your study goals and the grades you want.

The Sunday Study Review consists of six questions. Use your answers to propel you forward in your next study sessions.

1. Are you on track with your master study plan?
2. If not, what will you do to catch up?
3. What did you achieve last week? What went well?
4. What challenges did you overcome?
5. How successful was your studying? Did you study enough? Were you productive?
6. What changes could you introduce to make this week more successful?

Complete this exercise and then go straight into your weekly task planning to set yourself up for your most productive study week ever.

Action steps

- Complete the Best Study Self exercise.
- Distinguish between your Priority and Nice-to-Have study tasks each week.
- Schedule in your study sessions – don't leave them to chance!
- Download, print and test my Daily Study Session Planner for a week.
- Test the Pomodoro Technique for a week with a few different ratios.
- Complete The Sunday Study Review each week.

09
The dark side of productivity

It's time to talk about the things that can hold us back from being super, kick-butt productive and effective in our studies. This is the dark side of productivity: procrastination, tiredness, overwhelm and falling behind.

Why do we procrastinate?

First off, procrastination is a natural phenomenon. The rational part of your brain knows that studying now makes sense because it cares about your future success, but the emotional part of your brain couldn't give a hoot about the future because its sole goal is to maximize ease and pleasure *right now*. For example, you have an essay due next week that you should start tonight. But instead you watch a few Instagram Stories, get sucked into a YouTube black hole, browse through some new books on Amazon, reorganize your sock drawer, clean the bathroom, look up the menu of that new restaurant in town, pluck your eyebrows, clean out your desk drawers… need I go on? For procrastinators, the emotional part of their brain often wins, so they put off studying until the last possible moment and then have to work in extreme panic with lots of guilt.

Why is procrastination dangerous?

When you procrastinate, the time you spend 'having fun' or 'being busy' is filled with guilt. That Netflix binge seems rebellious and great at first but then the guilt strikes because you know you should be studying. The time you spend cleaning the bathroom feels good because you're getting stuff done, but that knot in your stomach returns when you think about your unwritten essay.

Also, you can't reach your full potential if you always leave work to the last minute. Now some of you may be reading this and thinking, 'but Chloe, I actually work better under pressure'. I'll admit that there's nothing like a deadline to light a fire under your butt to get working. But if you leave important study tasks until the last minute, there simply isn't time to do your best work. If you start writing an essay the day before it's due, you probably won't have enough time to edit it fully, so you'll lose marks from avoidable mistakes. If you don't start revising for a big exam until a few days before, it's unlikely you'll be able to recall all the important information to answer the questions fully.

I've said unlikely because there will be students who are OK at 'winging it' sometimes and getting a good grade. However, what grades could you get if you gave yourself more time for your tasks?

And let's look at the bigger picture here. Not every important task in life has a deadline. What if you want to change careers, start a business, learn a language, write a book, or get fitter? There's no external deadline on these, so you may never achieve them if you've created a habit of always leaving things to the last minute. Break your addiction to adrenaline-fuelled panic in your studies, and you'll give yourself the best chance at achieving the success you're capable of.

The five-step anti-procrastination method

1 Recognize the warning signs

The first step to change is awareness of a problem, so I want you to recognize the warning signs that you're procrastinating. Some examples are:

- Leaving an item on your task list for ages, or moving it from list to list.
- Filling your time with low-priority, busy tasks, such as clearing out your sock drawer, or rewriting your notes to make them prettier.
- Stopping studying to respond to every phone and computer notification.

2 Work out why you're procrastinating

Once you've realized you're procrastinating, you need to work out why – because we can't tackle the problem without knowing the root cause. I've come up with six possible reasons you might be putting off studying, so look through this list and see which one (or two) matches your current procrastination mood.

Easily distracted

You know you're supposed to be studying but find yourself responding to e-mails and checking your phone when a notification comes in. Your mind wanders and you struggle to stay focused on studying for more than a few minutes.

Lack of motivation

You rarely feel motivated to start studying and you're starting to believe something's wrong with you. When you don't feel like studying you either sack it off completely, or you waste hours procrastinating first.

Overwhelmed and disorganized

You have so much to do that you just don't know what to tackle first or your to-do list feels so scary that you often just need a lie down on your bed to ignore it a little longer. Your to-do list includes big, hairy study tasks such as 'write an essay' that you don't know how to start and you procrastinate because you can't see the point in starting them during a short study session.

Unpleasant or boring task

You don't want to read your boring textbook or take notes on a reading that sends you to sleep and you don't understand. Parts of your degree (or other qualification) are boring and hard so you put off doing them until you *have* to get cracking.

Fear of mistakes or failure

You put off starting a study task because you're afraid you'll fail or not be that good. Or, you put off revision because you don't want to realize how little material you know. This fear means you leave things until the last minute and therefore don't perform at your best. But when you get a low mark you protect your feelings by saying, 'I would have done better if I'd tried harder and had more time.' Trying hard and failing is worse than not trying and failing so if you don't really try you can't really fail.

Fear also shows up as perfectionism for some students. I often pride myself on being a perfectionist… which is silly, really, because perfection is unobtainable. When you strive for perfection, it's easy to procrastinate through fear of not getting it 100 per cent right.

Low self-confidence/'I'm a bad student'

You often come up against study tasks where you don't know what to do and you feel out of your depth. You worry you're not a good enough student, so you procrastinate because you're stuck or it's too hard to struggle through.

This low confidence might stem from the belief that you're a 'bad' student, which you could have developed during previous study, or you might have even been told it or made to believe it by a teacher, parent or sibling. The belief that you're a bad student limits you and can cause you to procrastinate because you can't see the point of trying.

3 *Decide you want to stop procrastinating*

I can give you hundreds of incredible, proven strategies to conquer procrastination, but if you don't actually *want* to stop procrastinating then they'll never work. You might be thinking, 'Wait, what?! *Obviously* I want to stop procrastinating, that's why I'm reading this chapter!' Let me explain using something I've been struggling with for years and am only just getting better at now!

Up until very recently, I couldn't get out of bed without snoozing my alarm many, many times. The night before, I'd set my phone alarm for 6:30 am so I could do a yoga session before work. The next morning the alarm would go off and almost immediately I'd hit snooze. Nine minutes later I'd hit snooze again... and again... and again... often five or six times.

By snoozing my alarm I'd wasted an hour of my morning, missed my slot to practise yoga, felt groggy from pushing myself back into sleep, got to work later which meant I had to stay later... and just generally started off my day in a negative way.

I know how silly this sounds, especially when there are simple solutions. If I put my phone on the other side of the room, then I have to actually get out of bed to turn it off. I'd be angry and shocked, a bit like a cat that's been dunked unexpectedly in a bath, but I'd be up.

My point is, procrastination can only be tackled if you want what's on the other side of procrastination enough... and you're willing to give up your procrastination activity. This sounds simple enough, but procrastination skews your logic.

For my snoozing problem, putting my phone on the other side of the room meant I wouldn't be able to scroll through Instagram before I went to sleep, or in bed when I woke up. I had to stop and look at my behaviour to start thinking rationally and to start wanting to ditch procrastination.

Here's a studying example. You put off starting your essay because it's difficult and boring and it's much easier to clean the bathroom or watch Netflix. However, you hate that you leave your essay writing until the last minute because it's stressful, you have to stay up later and you end up with crappier grades than necessary.

You know that you'd get your essay done well and on time if you decided on a non-negotiable start date and removed distractions before you sat down to study. But you don't do this because you prefer to procrastinate. Of course you'd rather watch back-to-back episodes of your favourite TV show, go for a picnic with your friends, or have the longest-ever hot bath!

Until you accept this *want* to stay the same, this resistance to change, you will continue to procrastinate. Earlier, I told you that the first step to change is awareness that you need to change. Well, most students stop at this stage. We moan on Instagram that we *need* to stop procrastinating and we *need* to achieve higher grades – most of the e-mails I get each day revolve around this issue. But when I give solutions, people dismiss them, because they don't *want* to implement them. They don't want to stop binging on Netflix at the weekend. They don't want to shut down Facebook when they study. They don't want to study without their phone next to them.

> **Try this – procrastination reflection**
>
> Grab a piece of paper and a pen and note down your answers to the following questions:
>
> 1 What study task are you putting off and procrastinating over?
> 2 What are the dangers of continuing to procrastinate? What is putting off 'X' study task stopping you from doing, being or achieving?
> 3 What are the benefits of doing the hard thing? What awesome stuff is on the other side of procrastination?
>
> Hopefully, once you've answered these questions you'll understand what's holding you back from finally conquering procrastination, and you'll be ready to give up doing what's easy and start doing what's harder (at first) to get what you want.

4 Implement the right anti-procrastination strategies

Now it's time to implement the right strategies that are best suited to your reason for procrastination. I've taken each of the six reasons for putting off studying and matched it with the best strategies for you to implement to kick it to the curb and boost your productivity.

Easily distracted

1 Set yourself up for success Follow the process in Chapter 7 to help you prepare for a productive study session: clear your desk; grab everything you'll need; grab some snacks; make yourself comfortable; find a soundtrack; and, most importantly, remove distractions. If you know you're easily distracted it's *your* responsibility to do something about it – so do whatever you need to do to your devices to stop them holding you back from the grades you deserve.

2 Use the Pomodoro Technique This method helps you stay focused, with its instructions to study your butt off and do nothing else for 25 minutes. Don't forget to use the procrastination list too to help you avoid getting distracted. Record any random thoughts that come into your head on a sticky note and then get straight back to it.

3 Single task instead of multitask We talked in Chapter 8 about how trying to multitask wastes your precious time. Instead, try to single task instead by working on one task only until it's done.

Lack of motivation

1 Disrupt your pattern You learned in Chapter 5 about how changing your state can improve your motivation. So, dance to your favourite song, quickly walk round the block or drink a glass of water to disrupt your pattern and make it easier to sit down at your desk and work.

2 Complete a 'no excuse' study task Successful students study, even when they don't want to. Therefore, when you're lacking motivation, pick a 'no excuse' study task (see Chapter 5) and get it done. You'll feel proud of yourself and will have gained the momentum you need to keep going.

3 Celebrate your achievements If you don't feel like you're making progress then your motivation is going to wane. To perk it back up, note down every study task you complete, big or small, so you have a list at the end of each study session. This should remind you that even when you feel like you're not making progress, every step forwards counts.

Overwhelmed and disorganized

1 Prioritize When you've got a gazillion tasks pressing down on you, work out your priorities. Work backwards from your next due date, and identify your needle-moving study tasks, the things you need to do now that will have the biggest impact. Start there.

2 Break the task down Split your larger tasks into smaller ones to make them more manageable and chase away the urge to procrastinate. 'Write an essay' becomes 'set up document', 'break down question', 'plan out sections', 'research articles', 'write the introduction', etc.

3 Single task instead of multitask See point above for 'easily distracted'.

Unpleasant or boring task

1 Use the Pomodoro Technique See point above for 'easily distracted'.

2 Eat the frog first As in Chapter 6, identify which hard or tedious task you've been procrastinating over and do that first. You'll feel happier afterwards, it may not have been as bad as you thought, and all your next tasks will seem easier in comparison.

3 Pick a study reward Choose a post-study treat before you start studying, to motivate yourself to do the work. Reward yourself for productivity and procrastination won't stand a chance.

Fear of mistakes or failure

1 Forgive yourself Carleton University psychology professor Michael J A Wohl and his colleagues conducted a study to look at the effect of self-forgiveness on procrastination (Wohl et al, 2010). They found that students who forgave themselves for procrastinating in the past were less likely to procrastinate in the future. Therefore, don't beat yourself up for slacking off; instead, turn a fresh page, forgive yourself and move forward with more productivity.

2 Ask for help   You should always attempt a problem yourself first, but if you've been struggling to understand a tricky concept or how to approach your next essay – ask. Don't waste time being stuck when you could reach out to your tutor and get that little bit of guidance to propel you forward.

3 Reframe failure and success   This isn't an instant fix, but try to nudge yourself into this mindset when your fear and procrastination strike. Try to assign feelings of success to situations where you've worked really hard and persevered. This makes mistakes unimportant, because as long as you put the *effort* in, your work (and you) are a success. And as we learned in Chapter 5, making mistakes is a necessary part of learning.

Low self-confidence/'I'm a bad student'

1 Ask for help   See point above for 'fear of mistakes or failure'.

2 Start with a quick win   Procrastination thrives when you doubt yourself, so fight back by picking a study task you know you can do. Start your studying with a simple, quick win to get the ball rolling and boost your confidence to continue with more complex tasks.

3 Celebrate your achievements   See point above for 'lack of motivation'.

5 *Get out of your head and into action*

Knowing *how* to beat procrastination, and *wanting* to stop procrastinating are great… but for some of you, an additional step is needed. Studying for a degree or similar qualification takes a long time, which means you need to actively *not* procrastinate hundreds, if not thousands, of times.

Leadership and motivation expert Mel Robbins explains that our emotions play a huge role in our productivity. How often have you thought, 'I need to study this weekend, but I don't *feel* like sitting at my desk all day'? Or, 'I should go for a run, but I don't *feel* like it.' Or, for me, 'I want to get to work early, but I don't *feel* like getting out of bed right now.'

Mel explains that when we leave time between deciding to do the hard thing (like studying) and actually doing it, our feelings rush to fill the gap. Because I don't *feel* like getting out of bed, I don't. If you decide you don't *feel* like studying, then you'll probably start procrastinating.

Enter, the 5 Second Rule. Mel Robbins (2017) explains, 'If you have an impulse to act on a goal, you must physically move within five seconds or your brain (and your feelings) will kill the idea.' This simple but powerful technique overrides bad habits by activating your pre-frontal cortex and acting as a 'starting ritual' to help you take control of your actions.

When you decide to study you must immediately count down from five and then get up and go. Let's say you go through the first four steps of the anti-procrastination process and you realize your strategy should be 'start with a quick win', say aloud, 'five, four, three, two, one' and immediately get to work on that first, small task.

This may sound too simple – but I promise you, it can be a game changer! Action is procrastination's kryptonite, so use the 5 Second Rule to get moving and conquer it.

How to deal with overwhelm

Do you ever feel like your brain is just too full? You have a bazillion study tasks and non-study tasks to complete, you're being pulled in a million different directions, and there's not enough time in the day. Your head's so full of stuff that you think you might forget it all if you sneeze.

I experience overwhelm *a lot* and it's not pretty. When I'm overwhelmed, I feel like a failure because I'm not doing great at anything. I'm not being a good student, a good employee, a good business owner, a good homemaker… girlfriend… daughter… friend… sister… ARGHHH!

Here are some strategies that help me (and will help you) step out from under the heavy cloud of overwhelm.

The brain download

When you feel overwhelmed, take a few slow, deep breaths and grab some paper and pens. Start by writing in the centre of your page 'all my thoughts' and then draw a bubble around it – this is now the centre of your brain download mind map.

Draw lines from the central bubble for each of the areas of your life where you're experiencing overwhelm, eg studying, work, family, home life, business, health, relationship, friends, etc.

Now, download everything that's clogging up your brain. Every task, event, worry – write them down around the appropriate bubble. Your brain download may look a little scary once you've finished… but you should find it easier to breathe now that your overwhelm is out of your head and onto paper.

If overwhelm is a common feeling, create a brain download every week as the first step in your planning process. Use your brain download as the ideas machine for creating your organized, prioritized, weekly to-do list.

The 5Ds

Grab another piece of paper and separate it into five sections: Do It, Delay It, Delegate It, Ditch It, and Do It Less Well. Add the tasks from your brain download under the relevant heading.

Do It tasks are your priorities, the tasks that are tapping you urgently on the shoulder – such as pay a bill, or finish your essay which is due in two days.

Delay It tasks are things you need to do, but they're not that urgent. Yes, you may need to buy your friend a present, but if their birthday's not until next month then your looming essay should be the priority (sorry procrastination!). Or you may want to create flashcards for your exam next month, but you have an essay due this week, so the flashcards can be delayed. Work out the tasks that can wait a while, and then schedule in a time to tackle them. Make sure not to forget this important half-step – add a slot into your diary to do them. Don't simply say you'll do it later (you won't! We're in a chapter about procrastination, after all!).

Delegate It tasks are those that don't need to be completed by you and that others could help with. Now, unfortunately we can't delegate our study tasks – but we can ask for support for lots of other things. Look at your brain download list and see if you can call in any favours from your family or friends to take some of these off you. Can your partner or housemate take on more of the cooking or cleaning responsibilities? If you have children, could they help out more with chores? Could a family member babysit, or ferry them around to after-school clubs? Everyone's situation is different, but see if you can delegate some tasks – even just temporarily – to create some breathing space.

Ditch It tasks are those you can remove completely from your list. Maybe they seemed like a great idea at the time, but they're kind of unrealistic now.

Perhaps you wanted to rewrite some of your notes because they're untidy – but actually, that won't help you get marks, so you can ditch this task.

The final category is **Do It Less Well**. Now, I'm not an advocate for submitting assignments where you know you could have done better. But when life gets crazy, something's gotta give – and it had better be your perfectionism rather than your sanity. Look at your list and be realistic about where you could afford to give a B- or C-grade effort. Rather than complete detailed notes for your entire textbook, look forward at your upcoming essays and then skim read any sections that aren't directly related.

If we all had unlimited hours in the day, we could afford to give maximum time, effort and energy to all areas of our lives. But sadly, Harry Potter-style Time Turners aren't real, so be realistic about your tasks and priorities to beat overwhelm.

How to study when you're tired

You know the feeling, right? You're trying to study, but your brain feels fuzzy and your eyelids are drooping. You have tasks to complete, but you feel like you've had a long *year*, not just a long day. It's hard to study when you're tired, but tiredness doesn't have to be a stopper for your productivity; it's still possible to do great work if you're sleepy.

First you need to work out your level of tiredness. Look at the options in the grid below and work out which best describes your situation right now.

Table 9.1 Studying when tired

	You should study but the world won't end if you don't	**You *really* have to study, ie essay or exam in a few days**
Tired, unmotivated, feel a bit 'meh'	Decide whether to take the day off and make time up later	Wake yourself up and study
Exhausted, would cry if you had the energy	Rest today to come back feeling more refreshed tomorrow	Talk to your tutor about a small extension. If not, or you have an exam, wake yourself up, prioritize your tasks and study

Six strategies for studying when you're tired

Wake yourself up

Take a shower; drink a large glass of water; make a cup of tea or coffee; get some fresh air; do five minutes of housework; put some loud music on or sing or dance around.

Do the easy things

When you're sleepy, you're going to struggle to do tasks that require a lot of brain power. If you're too tired to write an essay or take notes, think about the tasks you can do that require less brain power. For example, you could set up the document for your next essay, file your notes or work out your priority tasks for the week.

You could even do personal or household chores so that later today or tomorrow, you can study for longer. When my house is a mess, I struggle to concentrate, so sometimes I use my tired time to tidy and do laundry which means my studying that evening is more productive.

Study with more breaks

If you're really struggling, then adjust the Pomodoro Technique to have slightly longer breaks. Instead of studying for 25 minutes and taking a five-minute break (25/5), you could try 25/15 or 45/20. Use your breaks to get some fresh air or move around, rather than sitting down scrolling through Instagram, and you'll find it easier to keep studying.

Take a nap

I'm not a napper at all because I can't be trusted. I set my alarm for 20 or 30 minutes and when it goes off I just go back to sleep! But... a lot of people swear by taking power naps so if that's you, a short nap should replenish your energy so you can study effectively later.

Study with your energy

If you regularly feel tired when you're studying, try and adapt your study routine to fit your own natural energy rhythm. If you have more energy in the morning, study then, but if you're more energetic in the evenings then schedule your study sessions for later in the day.

Are you doing too much?

Lastly, if you always feel tired and rushed, ask yourself whether you're doing too much. It's normal to feel like you want it all, but we can't have everything we want in life at the same time. To avoid burnout, reflect on what's important to you in your life *right now* so you can prioritize the right things.

How to catch up when you've fallen behind

It's not a fun moment when you look at your schedule or syllabus and realize you're behind. If you study while working, then finding extra hours to catch up can seem impossible – so I want to share with you my best strategies for getting back on track.

Identify your priorities

Look at your due dates to see what essays and/or exams you have coming up. If you haven't got any for a few weeks, follow the rest of these strategies. If you do, then look at how important these assessments are. If you have an essay due that's worth 10 per cent of your module grade, then a lower mark for this is not as disastrous as getting a lower mark for an essay worth 30–40 per cent of your final grade. Understand the importance of your assignments so you can work out how severe your get-back-on-track efforts should be.

Ask for an extension

If you have an essay due and you're trying to catch up but don't think you will in time, then it's worth asking your tutor for a small extension. Go to them with a plan of when you think you can submit and what you're going to do to make it happen. The worst thing that can happen is they say no; the best thing is that they give you time to submit work you're proud of.

Seek support for tough concepts

If you fall behind because you struggle to understand your materials, then don't be afraid to reach out for help from your tutor. They should be able to help you face-to-face, by phone or by e-mail – they could explain a concept differently, give you a new technique or point you in the direction of additional resources.

Seek further support if you're really struggling

If you're seriously struggling and considering giving up, then reach out to your university or college first. Contact them and find out your options; you might be able to defer a module and take a break for a few months (or as long as you need) before coming back.

Talk to your support network

It's important to have someone to talk to about your studying, who you can share your wins with but who will also listen to your overwhelmed rants when needed. Reach out to those in your circle or see if you can connect with other students on your course (in real life or virtually), so that you're not alone on this journey.

Free up time

In order to catch up on your studies you'll have to free up some time, so look at your calendar for the next few weeks and see where you can create space by moving, deleting or changing some of your events, appointments and other commitments.

When things got crazy in my study life, I rearranged my social plans and told all my friends and family not to disturb me for the foreseeable future!

Be kind to yourself

Try not to dwell on the fact you're behind. It can be easy to slip into 'I'm a rubbish student' thoughts, but these won't put you in the frame of mind needed to get back on track. Yes, you've fallen behind; no, you're not a failure.

Be kind to yourself. Everyone gets off track sometimes; what's more important is that you've decided to work hard and catch up.

Don't forget to take breaks

When you're behind, it can feel like you haven't even got time to pee, let alone take a break… but we know from Chapter 8 that small, regular study breaks are needed to maintain focus and productivity over long study sessions. The Pomodoro Technique will help you stay focused and achieve more in less time.

Identify why you fell behind

And finally, reflect on why you fell behind in the first place. Did you struggle with the material? Did you procrastinate over starting your essay or revision? Did you spend too long relaxing or socializing? Did you forget to plan, so all your due dates crept up? Ask yourself questions like these to work out what you can do to make sure you stay on track in future.

Self-care over burnout

Psychologist Herbert Freudenberger (1974) coined the term 'burnout' to describe the state of mental and physical exhaustion caused by 'excessive demands on energy, strength, or resources' in professional life. Symptoms include fatigue, headaches, difficulty sleeping, low motivation, cynicism and negativity, among others. I'm not telling you about burnout so that you can diagnose yourself, but so that you can see the possible dangers of studying too hard for too long.

I am a definite advocate for working hard and studying alongside other commitments, but to make sure we reap the benefits, and don't get burned out, we need to pull back and recuperate when we get the chance. Whenever you do have a break in your studying, whether it's a few months, weeks, or even days, take some time out so you can come back refreshed, happier and more motivated.

The way to pull back is by practising self-care. Self-care is a spectrum which also involves medical care, but I want to talk to you about it from an individual, wellbeing sense of how to practise self-care during your studies.

I believe there are two elements of self-care – looking after yourself and replenishing yourself. Looking after yourself means doing the simple but essential things to maintain your health and happiness: eating healthy food, drinking enough water, getting a good amount of sleep and moving your body, for example. We all know we *should* be doing these things, but when we've got our heads down and we're stuck in essay-writing or exam revision mode it's easy to ditch them.

I think most of us accept that we feel calmer and more energetic when we look after ourselves, so let's make a commitment together that we'll try to care for ourselves every day. When our studying eases up, we can switch our focus to topping up these areas, so we can perform at our best and keep our energy and motivation high for longer.

The second element of self-care is replenishing yourself, and this means doing the things that make you feel happy, calm and energized. Now these things are different for everyone but, as an idea, here are the self-care tasks that replenish me:

- Painting my nails while watching the TV show *Grand Designs*.
- Sitting in silence for a few minutes while drinking a pot of mint tea.
- Singing so loudly in the car it hurts.
- Re-reading cards I've received from my family and best friends.

Identify what replenishes *you* and make time for it.

Now, you might think you don't have time to just spend on yourself because you have a job, or maybe a family to look after. But self-care is like that emergency rule on an aeroplane where you must put your own oxygen mask on before helping others. If you're in danger you can't help others; if you're stressed and unhappy you can't work at your best or support your loved ones fully.

Try to practise self-care during your studies, and definitely embrace it when you have study breaks, so you can be a happier and calmer student and human.

Finally, here are two ways you can pull back and relax when you have study breaks.

1 Spend time on your worn-out areas

Think about the areas in your life that have become a bit tired while you've been in crazy study mode. However, there's no blame allowed here. I'm not asking you to do this so you can beat yourself up about all the ways you're not good enough. We can't give 100 per cent effort to everything in life at the same time so it's completely natural for some areas to slip while you're working your butt off in your studies.

Decide on some areas you're going to spend a little bit more time on to improve your wellbeing. For me, this always means decluttering my house, batch cooking some healthy food, and getting back into an exercise routine.

2 Embrace white space

Plans and structure are necessary when you're in get-stuff-done mode in your studies, but can be a shackle when you're trying to pull back and relax.

Try to have days where you have white space, where you don't have every hour allocated.

Also, make an effort to add silence to your day. I seem to have got into a habit of filling every spare minute of my day with music, an audiobook, or a podcast episode. This means I've slipped out of being able to appreciate silence and the benefits it can bring such as clarity, peace and creative thinking. Make a point of having times in your day where you do nothing and listen to nothing.

Action steps

- If you're procrastinating:
  - Work out why you're procrastinating.
  - Pick the best anti-procrastination strategy and use the 5 Second Rule to go, go, go!
- If you're overwhelmed:
  - Complete a brain download and categorize with the 5Ds.
- If you've fallen behind:
  - Identify your priorities.
  - Talk to your tutor if you need an extension, don't understand something or need further support.
  - Create space in your schedule.
  - Work out why you fell behind.
- If you're tired:
  - Work out whether you should push on and study or pull back and rest.
  - Wake yourself up.
  - Complete easier tasks.
  - Take more breaks.
- Make time for self-care by embracing white space and paying attention to the areas of your life where you're worn out.

Part Four
Classes, note taking and assignment skills

10
Classes

Two elements make up the learning in most courses: independent study and direct teaching during classes. The ratio of these two elements varies wildly depending on the subject and format of each course. For example, degrees in science subjects are likely to have more hours per week of lectures or tutorials than a humanities subject. Then, distance learning courses are likely to offer fewer direct teaching hours, because flexibility is a key need of their students – and this need is best served through independent, learn-when-it-suits-you study.

Now, there are a lot of terms thrown around when it comes to classes, so I want to start by explaining what each of these means – with a caveat that these terms will vary by university or college, so make sure you work out the format and aims of *your* classes.

> **Glossary**
>
> **Lecture.** A lecture is a formal, one-sided class where you and other students sit, listen and take notes while a teacher or guest speaker gives a presentation or talks about a specific topic. A lecture is information-heavy, so there may be little to no time for asking questions, and note taking or recording, if allowed, is essential.
>
> **Tutorial.** A tutorial, sometimes called a seminar or workshop, is a smaller, more interactive class where discussion is expected. They may be based on lecture topics and could include group work, Q&A, presentations or activities. For a tutorial, you will often be asked to prepare by completing some pre-reading, activities or research.
>
> **Office hours.** Office hours are informal, one-on-one sessions your tutor may provide where you can drop in or book an appointment to ask for specific help with your studies.

> **Practical.** A practical is a hands-on, skills-based class used in some subjects such as science or engineering, taught in labs, or arts subjects, taught in studios.

If you study at a traditional, full-time, bricks-and-mortar university or college, then you'll likely experience most of these different types of classes. If you are a distance learner, then you'll likely learn mainly through independent self-study – but you may also have tutorial-style online classes, and you'll probably either have online office hours, or be told to contact your tutor as and when you need help. When I studied at the Open University I had around one tutorial a month, and I could choose to travel to a face-to-face class or attend an online version.

The importance of attending classes

Obviously, it's important to attend a class where you're being taught new material because your knowledge on this material is what will be tested in your essays and exams. Some classes won't teach you new material, so you may wonder if that means you can safely skip it – the short answer to this is no! During lectures, new material is shared and references made to your upcoming essays or exams, and the key material you'll need to understand to do well. Tutorials use discussion and activities to help you deepen your knowledge and understanding of the material, which will help you write better essays and improve your recall for exams. They also allow you to learn from and bounce ideas off other students, and give you a chance to check your understanding of concepts and ask your tutor questions.

As the incredible independent learner I know you to be, you'll know that you alone are responsible for your education, and if you don't actively engage in it then you're wasting your time, energy and money investment. Successful students make every effort to attend all their classes so they can give themselves the best chance. I was told by one of my first Open University tutors that, on average, in her class, the students who attended her classes achieved 10 per cent higher grades than those who didn't – now who wouldn't want an extra 10 per cent in their essay and exam marks?!

How to get the most out of your classes

Successful students know they'll get more value out of their classes if they prepare for them. Here are some key reasons why you should complete the assigned prep work:

- You will deepen your understanding by relearning material that's already familiar.
- You might miss important points if you spend the entire class trying to digest and take notes on new material.
- You can ask intelligent questions rather than those answered later in the material.
- You will have free brain space to consider how the material relates to the real world or other concepts you've learned.
- In tutorials, you will feel more confident when discussing theories and ideas.
- In tutorials, you will have more opportunity to engage with your tutor and fellow students because you're not in 100 per cent absorption mode.

How to prepare for class

Understand the class aim(s)

Look in your course information or ask your tutor what the aim of the lecture or tutorial is. A lecture may be about teaching new material, whereas a tutorial may be geared towards giving you deeper understanding of familiar material, guidance for your next assignment, or a revision session.

Check your study plan

Look at your study plan or syllabus to check what due dates you have coming up. If you have an essay due soon that is related to the subject of your class, then spend 10 minutes checking your understanding of the question or topic. If you have any questions, bring them to class and either ask them directly or listen up for mention of key points to include or other additional guidance.

Double-check the logistics

Make sure you find out when and where your class will be and check the day before to make sure this hasn't changed. Also, identify what you should bring to class; for example, printouts of readings, textbooks, notes, or answers to pre-questions.

Do the prep work

For a lecture you might be asked to complete some background reading related to the lecture subject, and for a tutorial you may be asked to complete an activity or quiz, prepare a short presentation, or take notes on a reading you will dive into during class.

When completing your pre-reading, make note of any theories or ideas that you don't understand. Then you can ask your tutor a question about these ideas during or after class, or make sure you're paying extra-special attention when the area is covered.

Find out the in-class materials

A lot of tutors will share the handouts or slides after class, and some may even upload a recording of the class. It's important to find out the additional resources you'll be given so you know how in-depth your class notes should be – key points, details, examples or a full summary – and what you'll be able to add after class.

Tell your tutor if you can't make it

If you have good reason to miss a class, then make sure you tell your tutor. It shows them respect, but also allows you to ask for any resources that will help you catch up.

How to act during class

Be the nerdy kid

Never be afraid to be a teacher's pet. For a face-to-face class, turn up early, greet your tutor, sit at the front, answer questions and thank them afterwards. Firstly, you'll impress them; secondly, it's nice to be nice; and thirdly, you'll find it easier to see and hear what's going on. You can still do this for an online class – log on a few minutes early, participate fully and send your tutor a quick e-mail to thank them after the class.

Don't write down everything

It's pretty much impossible to write down all the class material, especially during a lecture. It's likely you'll have to complete your notes after class, so focus instead on writing down key points and additional ideas and concepts not included in the handouts or shown on the slides. It's also worth asking your tutor if you can record the audio of all or part of the class so you can complete your notes afterwards. Be sure to never record a class without permission.

Engage

I can't imagine anything worse than teaching a class of students who don't want to be coaxed out of silence. Do yourself and your tutor a favour by participating, even if you'd rather be horizontal at home scoffing chocolate! Join in group discussions and offer answers when your tutor asks a question – which will also help you improve your understanding. If you have any questions about the material, and questions are welcome in the class, ask them! You never know… there may be other, shyer students who have the same question, but are too afraid to speak up.

Stay focused

Contact hours are precious, so don't waste them scrolling through social media – there are enough hours in the day for that as it is! Make a commitment to yourself and your education by doing whatever you can to stay focused in class. Put your phone away, save chit-chat with other students until after class, and if you find your mind wandering, bring it back to the lesson.

What to do after class

Thank them

This could be a simple 'thanks professor' as you leave, or you could send them an e-mail. Extra bonus points for you if you tell them what ideas you found the most interesting, or the most helpful for your studies.

Ask questions

The class may have introduced some tricky concepts you didn't quite grasp, or stirred up some questions you have about the material or its broader application. If so, stay after class, book an appointment, or send an e-mail to your tutor and ask these questions. Just a little bit more guidance can improve your understanding, which can have a big impact on your grades.

Complete your notes

Take the notes you made during class, and any handouts or slides from your tutor, and finish off a clear set of notes that you understand and can use to help you with your essay writing and exam revision.

Class troubleshooting

Here are some tips for common problems you might encounter during classes.

Other students aren't engaging

I remember going to a tutorial for one of my marketing modules and the tutor kept asking the class questions, and I was the *only* student to put my hand up and offer an answer. I didn't always get it right but after answering two or three questions I felt I should stop putting my hand up because I was worried that I was drawing attention to myself.

But then I thought, why do I care what anyone else thinks? Every minute of this tutorial has cost me money... so why would I sit in silence just because I don't want people to think I'm a nerd? From then on, I *always* engaged in class – even if no one else was – and I want you to do the same.

The tutor doesn't cover the upcoming, important essay or exam

When you have a tutorial a week or so before an essay or exam is due, it would be really helpful if your tutor spent some time answering questions or giving additional guidance to support you. In most of my tutorials, this *did* happen, but in some of them it didn't, and I'd leave feeling annoyed and like my time would have been better spent essay writing or revising at home.

However, as independent learners we have to take control of our own education, and this means sometimes asking for what we need. What I started doing (and you can too if you notice this issue) was e-mailing my tutor the week of the class and asking if they could carve out some time specifically to talk about the essay or exam. The worst thing that can happen is they say no! If they *do* say no, then move to Plan B, but also keep asking before your tutorials and ask your fellow students to do the same. If enough of you ask for it, your tutor should listen. Plan B, in the meantime, is to arrive at your tutorial early or stay late so you can ask any questions related to your essay or exam.

You don't find the class interesting or useful

First, we need to reality-check this one because, unfortunate newsflash, not everything in studying and life is going to be interesting. But if you really believe the lecture or tutorial wasn't valuable, what could you do about it? I'd recommend going to your tutor and politely and respectfully telling them what you *would* love to see in the next class. Your tutors aren't mind readers, so give them specifics of what would be helpful for you.

You're struggling to maintain concentration

The best way to keep focused in class is to focus on active engagement. I had a few tutorials where I thought I was going to fall asleep, so I solved this by taking off a jumper to cool down, drinking some water, and note taking. The act of writing down and trying to summarize my tutor's points helped me regain concentration. Other strategies include putting your phone away, and asking and answering questions.

You can't keep up

If your tutor moves too fast for you to write points down, leave some space in your notes to fill in later, with the help of the handouts, your tutor or another student's notes.

You're stuck

If you don't understand something and you're in a tutorial, ask a question. If you're in a lecture, then write down your question to ask after class. I find it helpful to ask the tutor for context around the concept by describing an example or case study. Doing the prep work will help you get familiar with the ideas and give you a chance to notice your stuck points beforehand so you can do something about it.

Action steps

- Find out the aims of each of your class types.
- For your upcoming class:
  - Do the prep work.
  - Double-check the time and location.
  - Note down any questions you have or concepts you don't understand to bring up during class.
  - If you have an essay coming up, check your understanding and bring any questions to class.
  - Find out what material you will be given so you can decide on the depth of your in-class note taking.

11
Note taking

Effective note taking is a stepping stone to achieving great grades. The act of summarizing your study material helps you understand the ideas and note taking builds the connections in your brain needed to retrieve the information at a later date. When you're in an exam, your ability to recall your course material accurately will affect your final grade. Also, your notes become a permanent record of what you have read or heard – which is vital for your assessments. When you start writing an essay, you can use great notes to help you find relevant ideas and when you start preparing for exams, great notes form the initial material you'll use for revision.

Common note-taking mistakes

There are some key note-taking mistakes that I've made in the past, and that I see my clients make. If you read this and notice that you're making some of these mistakes – don't worry! Here's what to do instead.

1 *Not taking* any *notes*

There are some students who think they don't have to take notes. Some reasons I've heard are: 'I can borrow my friends' notes', 'the textbook has already written the ideas perfectly', 'I don't have time', or 'I'll just highlight my textbook'.

Unfortunately, these aren't good reasons – as reasonable as they may seem! To achieve high grades, you need to *understand* your course material… which is greatly helped by taking notes in some form.

Your textbooks have been written by authors who know the subject really well, so it may seem like browsing the textbook is sufficient. But creating your own record of what *you* think are the key points will help you as you move onto writing essays, creating presentations and revising for exams.

It may be tempting to borrow or copy your friends' notes, but this is unwise for three reasons: you don't know that they've covered all the key points; you don't know that they've noted down ideas accurately; and your understanding will be weaker because you're trying to form connections from material that your brain didn't create.

Note taking takes time, but it'll save you time later and help you achieve higher grades. You'll be able to start essay writing with improved understanding of the material and an idea of relevant points to include. And starting revision with a good set of notes is like starting a marathon from the half-way mark – because you'll have started the recall process and will have ready-made revision material.

Bear in mind, too, that simply highlighting lines in your textbooks is a mindless study activity. It *feels* useful… and it's pretty satisfying to turn your textbook pages into a rainbow. But if you *just* highlight your textbooks, and don't turn this into your own notes, then you're wasting your time.

2 Making verbatim notes

Successful students know that they must write notes in their own words where possible, rather than simply copying them verbatim from the textbooks.

The mental processes involved in verbatim note taking are minimal:

Read information > copy information

When you write notes in your own words, your brain is engaging in a lot more processes:

Read information > process information > understand ideas > analyse value of information > link ideas with existing knowledge > create new, personalized explanation

When you write in your own words, you have to *understand* the ideas to be able to make judgements as to their value. You'll take into consideration your existing knowledge before you create your own summary. This process may take longer, but it will *skyrocket* your learning. Essay writing and exam revision will be easier, because you have a higher level of understanding and recall of the material.

3 Simply summarizing

As you progress through your studies, you'll be expected to critique what you're reading, draw your own conclusions and link between concepts.

One way to develop your critical thinking skills is by adding your own thoughts to your notes, either in the margins, in the text itself, or at the end of each section. These thoughts may include:

- strengths and weaknesses of the theories;
- contrasting theories or models;
- examples or case studies;
- ideas for translating theory to practice;
- reflections and what you've learned;
- links to other course concepts;
- links to your previous knowledge.

Taking great notes

Now you've learned what *not* to do, I want to dive deeper into the *how* behind great note taking, starting with the two key questions you need to ask yourself before you start.

The first question to ask yourself is, *what will my notes be used for?* For each module, identify the types of assessments you'll be given; note taking in preparation for essay writing is different to note taking in preparation for exams.

For modules with essays, take notes with each essay question in mind. You want a broad understanding of the key ideas you're being taught, as well as giving special attention to the concepts that are relevant for your essays. Add your own thoughts to your notes – this will help speed up the essay-writing process, as well as engage your critical thinking muscles to nab those higher marks. You may be able to save time on your note taking by only writing brief notes on the areas that aren't directly relevant to your essays.

Note taking is more important if you're studying modules with exams. In one of my business modules, I fell behind with note taking throughout the year… and this really bit me in the butt during my revision. We were only given three weeks to revise, and I had to spend a large part of that filling in the gaps in my notes. I didn't have good material to start my revision from, which meant I had less time to spend on memorizing the material, testing my knowledge and practising my exam techniques. My exam grade was lower than I wanted, and after I stopped moping, I realized I'd learned a valuable lesson – to commit to creating great notes *throughout* my studying, to give me a head start on my revision.

Focus your note taking for exams on understanding and summarizing the key points of the material. If you come to a confusing section, don't skip ahead, but instead look for new explanations online or ask your tutor for help.

Next you need to ask yourself, *am I trying to take notes during class or during independent study?* In my experience, note taking happens in two parts: absorption and sense-making. During independent study, these elements happen concurrently. You read a paragraph, watch a video, or listen to an audio clip; you absorb its meaning; then you make sense of it as you write your notes. This means that you'll probably find it easier to take notes during independent study: you can stop, start and go back until you're happy.

During classes, your tutor will often move too quickly for you to be able to create notes in your own words – the sense-making part. In fast-paced lectures, it's tempting to try and write down everything that's said – but this often means you're writing verbatim, which we know isn't useful, and you'll miss key points from not being able to handwrite or type quickly enough.

This presents a problem that has a few solutions. Some students try and take notes in class that include all the main points, but trying to combine sense making and absorption (like you do in independent study) can result in doing both less well. These students need to go back, check their understanding and rewrite their notes, adding in their own thoughts and any points they missed.

Other students accept that their notes during class aren't going to be that useful, so they instead focus on absorption. They listen actively and note down only the interesting points, useful examples and extra details not included on the slides. After class, they create a great set of notes in their own words using their own jottings and all the handouts.

Some tutors record their classes, so their students can check their understanding and improve their notes later. If your tutor doesn't do this, then you could ask them if they mind you recording the audio on your phone. I've done this before in a lecture, but my tutor asked me to stop the recording for the interactive parts with other students. It was really helpful to have this resource to listen to after class during the sense-making part of my note taking.

Note-taking location clues

Here are some nifty clues to help you identify where to find the important stuff that needs recording as notes:

- *Learning aims or outcomes* – find these in your course guidance, list them at the front of your folder and refer to them as you take notes. In one of my business modules I was tasked with studying competitive strategy. One of the learning outcomes was *to understand the methods in which an organization decides their competitive strategy*. When taking notes on the competitive strategy chapter in my textbook, I made sure I followed this clue and recorded the theories that would direct an organization to choose their competitive strategy.
- *Chapter introductions and conclusions/summaries* – typically, an introduction sets out what you will be taught and a conclusion or summary recaps what you should now know. After you've taken your notes for each chapter, reread the introduction and conclusion to double-check you've included all the key points, or read these sections *before* you start your note taking, to help you identify the key areas.
- *Essay questions* – identify the essay topic, find the relevant source material then pinpoint the relevant concepts and ideas. Write these on a sticky note and keep it close to you as you take notes. Taking notes through the lens of your next essay question will help you focus and will make your essay writing easier as your brain is on the hunt for relevant points to include in your essay.
- *Practice and past exam questions* – look for any patterns in the questions or areas that come up as you'll then know to take more detailed notes on these concepts or theories.
- *Class agenda or structure* – this will help you stay on track, anticipate the next points and find your place if you catch yourself daydreaming for a minute!
- *Points repeated or emphasized by your tutor.*
- *Signposts in your tutor's speech* – listen out for these to indicate the direction of the material. Some examples are:
  - 'I will now discuss…'
  - 'Another point is…'
  - 'My next point is…'

- 'On the other hand…'
- 'Others have argued that…'
- 'The evidence for this is…'
- 'An example of this is…'

Note-taking content clues

Most textbooks are written in an academic tone, which can sometimes be pretty confusing. I don't know about you, but I've often had to reread long sentences, unsure of what's being said. Secondly, textbooks can sometimes feel quite bloated, like it takes them a long time to say something. This is done for good reason, though; the more details, background, context and examples an author can give, the higher the chance the reader will understand the ideas.

This means that we as students have to work a bit harder sometimes to decipher the key nuggets of information to record as notes. Here's a list you can use to quickly identify the important stuff:

- *Definitions and explanations of a term/theory/concept* – what is its basic description?
- *Origins of a term/theory/concept* – who came up with it? What is their background? Why did they create it?
- *Viewpoints or perspectives on a term/theory/concept* – is this theory agreed upon by most experts in its field? Are there different viewpoints? If so, what are they? Which are the most popular and why? What are the strengths and weaknesses of these varying perspectives?
- *Strengths and weaknesses of a term/theory/concept* – what are its advantages and disadvantages? Are there gaps or mistakes in the reasoning? Are there situations where it's not useful?
- *Rules, principles, models and diagrams* – examples in this book are my 'Seven Steps for Setting Epic Study Goals' or my 'Five-step Anti-procrastination Method'. Any ideas with numbered parts represent the meat of the content you are likely to be tested on in essays and exams.
- *Examples and case studies* – these help you comprehend complex ideas and your use of them in essay writing and exams demonstrates that you understand the material and can apply it to a situation.

If your note taking includes these elements, I'd bet that you'll be fine!

How to take notes

There are lots of complex methods out there for writing notes and scanning your textbooks for key ideas, but I believe in simplicity and intuition. No method will work for every student and subject, so instead, here is a logical process that you can tweak and implement using your own judgement.

Seven-step note-taking process

1 Look for guidance

Look at your list of learning outcomes and upcoming essay questions to identify sections where you want to focus your note taking.

2 Read the chapter cues

Read the introduction and conclusion/summary of the chapter to get a feel for the content.

3 Scan through a few paragraphs or pages

Quickly read a small section of the text. You'll need to use your judgement here on the length of text. 'One section' could be just a paragraph, or it could be a few pages. Use the subheadings and the text formatting (bolding, underlining, italics) as signposts.

4 Highlight key ideas

Using your list of note-taking content clues, highlight or underline what you think sounds important. Some paragraphs will be full of key information such as definitions, rules or strengths whereas others may include less important details or background information.

5 Add other ideas

Write down any relevant thoughts that come to you while reading – links to another theory or theorist's work, additional strengths or weaknesses, your own examples, reflections, contrasting viewpoints or concepts, etc. Either jot these down on a sticky note or add them into the margin of the textbook (assuming the textbook is yours to write on!).

6 Write your notes

Now it's time to create your notes, which may be brief or detailed depending on their purpose, eg essay-based or exam-based course (more on this shortly…).

7 Check for clarity and understanding

Double-check your notes using any relevant guidance you found (learning outcomes and essay question) and reread the introduction and conclusion to be sure you covered the key points. Read through your notes to see if *you* understand them. Work on any unsure bits and see if there are any gaps you should fill with another example or detail.

Effective note-taking methods

Here are my three go-to note-taking techniques, but remember, you can follow these strictly, adapt them to suit you or pick bits from each method to create your own.

Mind maps

A mind map is a visual method of illustrating ideas and concepts focused around a central idea, created by Tony Buzan (1974).

Mind maps are great for brainstorming ideas, planning an essay or identifying the links between concepts. I also use them to prepare for exams by creating one that includes all of the theories I need to learn during revision.

You create a mind map by taking a piece of paper and adding a central idea to the centre. Then you decide on the most important words or phrases that relate to the main idea and add them as branches shooting out from the

Figure 11.1   Mind map example

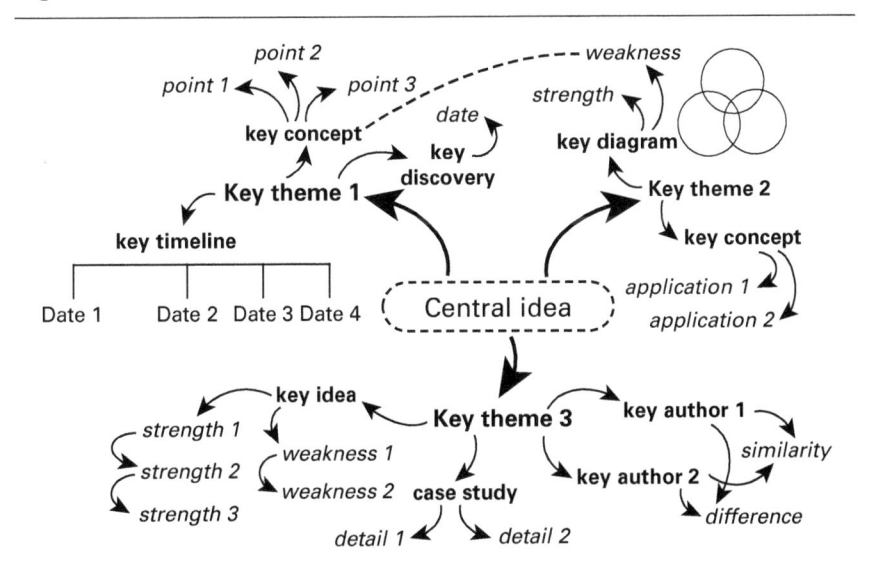

middle. Next, you take each of these branches and add more offshoots which you label with related information such as examples, authors, models, strengths, limitations, etc. Any ideas that are linked can be connected with further lines.

Mind map strengths

- Easy to fit a lot of information on one page.
- Great for creative, visual learners, as they can be personalised.
- Gain a deeper understanding of the material by identifying links between ideas.
- The short points can trigger recall of longer ideas.

Mind map limitations

- Can get messy quickly.
- Not as useful for large or wordy concepts.
- It can be hard to judge the space needed for each idea.
- Time-consuming – not as appropriate for lectures.

Tips for using mind maps

- Use blank paper, as lined can make your mind map look messy.
- Use different coloured pens and thicknesses of branches to differentiate ideas.
- Add diagrams or drawings to illustrate certain ideas.
- Add dotted lines to show connections between ideas.
- Mind maps can be created visually using apps – one I've used is Simple Mind+. They have a free mobile app with limited functionality, or a paid version where you can add images, sync them between devices and export them as images or PDFs. Another option is MindMeister, which has a free version that gives you a limited number of mindmaps, or a paid version with full functionality.

The Cornell method

The Cornell note-taking method was created in the 1950s by Cornell University professor, Walter Pauk. This technique condenses your material and prompts you to review and test your knowledge to deepen your understanding (Pauk and Owens, 2013). It's a useful method in modules that include exams, as your notes become your revision material – it's a win-win!

Figure 11.2 Cornell example

Date	Module/class	Topic

Cues	**Notes**
cue 1	
cue 2	
cue 3	
cue 4	
cue 5	

Summary

To use the Cornell method, take a piece of paper and draw a horizontal line about three-quarters of the way down the page – this becomes your 'summary' section. Then, draw a vertical line from the top of the page to the summary section, about a third of the way in from the left-hand side of the page. This left-hand section becomes your 'cue' column and the right-hand, larger section becomes your 'notes' column.

Take your notes in the notes column in any way you want. Your aim is to record the key points (you can use the note-taking content clues to help you identify these). Once you've finished, comb through your notes to find the key details and then formulate questions or prompts from these. For example, *the four principles of complexity theory* or, *what is the elevation of Mount Everest?* The aim here is to reduce your notes to essential ideas that can be expanded as you test your recall.

Lastly, condense your 'notes' column into a few sentences for the 'summary' section. Sum up the main ideas using the following questions to help you: why is this information important? What conclusions can I draw? In this section you'll create a brief overview of the topic which further deepens your understanding of the material.

When you want to revise with your notes, simply cover up the 'notes' and 'summary' and test yourself using the 'cues' column. See if you can expand upon the cues to give the answer or the full explanation. You can also cover up the 'cues' and 'notes' columns and test yourself by trying to add the details back into the information written in the 'summary' section.

Cornell strengths

- A neat method of organizing your notes.
- Flexible as you can take your actual notes however you want.
- Saves time, as your notes become your revision guides.
- You'll gain a deeper knowledge of the material by identifying cues and creating a summary.

Cornell limitations

- Relatively time-consuming.
- If you don't use the notes again, the extra effort in creating cues and a summary is wasted.
- Limited by space in the notes column.

Tips for using the Cornell method

- Use bullet points, symbols, diagrams and abbreviations to condense your notes.
- Leave a gap or draw a line between main ideas.
- If you want to write longer notes, try adding your 'summary' section only to your last page of notes for that section.

The Outlining method

This method organizes notes into hierarchies of related points separated by their importance. Main points are written to the left of the page and then sub-points and details are added in levels towards the right of the page.

This method can be used to create an essay plan where main ideas form the first level and supporting evidence, examples and critique form the lower, indented levels. It is also a good method for most subjects as it enables clear distinction between main ideas and details.

The typical levels of the Outlining method are: main topic; key concept; supporting detail. However, you may decide to add further levels to your note taking. On a new piece of a paper, or page of a digital document, start adding the information to the relevant level.

Outlining strengths:

- Quick and neat.
- Clearer than using block paragraphs.
- Easy to skim read to find key information.
- Can be used as a sub-technique inside the 'notes' section of the Cornell method.

Outlining limitations:

- Learning curve to work out correct levels.
- Can get messy if you make mistakes or need to add more.

Figure 11.3 Outlining example

Main Topic #1
    Key concept A
        Key author + date
        Example

    Key concept B
        Strength
        Limitation

Main Topic #2
    Key concept A
        Origin of concept
        Link to concept Z

    Key concept B
        Detail 1
        Detail 2

Tips for using the Outlining method:

- Create your own key for the levels.
- Use different colours for different levels.
- Leave space between each main topic so you can add more details later.

A blended approach

I recommend trying each of these methods for at least a week to give you time to test them and find what works for you. You might decide on one method, or you might decide to create your own. Maybe your current note-taking method is similar to Outlining – you could continue that, but add in Cornell-style cues to your margins to test your recall of the material later. Or perhaps you might switch to the Cornell style, but remove the summary section in order to keep your notes flexible.

Ultimately, I recommend a blended, flexible approach for note taking; in the last year of my degree I used all three methods. I created mind maps for planning my essays and mapping out topics for revision. In my essay-based module I used a variation of the Outlining method for day-to-day note taking and in my exam-based module I switched to the Cornell method so I could combine note taking with the creation of kick-butt revision guides.

Handwritten vs typed

A common question I'm asked by students is, *should I handwrite or type my notes?* There's no right or wrong answer, so have a look at the benefits of each, and make your own decision.

The benefits of handwriting your notes

- Some studies show students who handwrite their notes have a stronger understanding of the material than those who type their notes. Researchers Pam Mueller and Daniel Oppenheimer conducted three studies to determine the difference in effectiveness between handwriting and typing notes (Mueller and Oppenheimer, 2014). They discovered that students who typed their notes performed worse when quizzed about the content

of the class compared to students who handwrote their notes. Students who type their notes tend to transcribe their classes and write verbatim, whereas students who handwrite process and sort the material into their own words – which improves their understanding.
- Allows for creativity and personalization.
- Notes can be taken anywhere as long as you have paper.
- Many exams are still handwritten, which could present a challenge for a student who never gets any handwriting practice.
- Fewer distractions from a laptop.

The benefits of typing your notes

- Faster than handwriting (though make sure you take notes in your own words).
- Often neater than handwriting as mistakes can be fixed.
- It's easier to add more information or rearrange sections.
- Easy to back up and access wherever you are.
- Notes become searchable, which is useful for essay writing.

After reading these lists you may find it easy to make your decision – but some of you may still be unsure. My favourite approach is a blended method, to get the benefits of both. When you need to record your thoughts quickly then typing may make sense; for example, during a fast-paced lecture or when writing an essay.

But for condensing and understanding information you want to move slower to help you process and tease out the key material. Handwriting may be best on this occasion, or typed note taking where you are deliberate in refraining from simply copying the textbook word for word.

Initially, I hated the idea of mixing my note taking as I thought it would look messy, but I soon saw the value in tailoring my note taking to fit each situation. I would handwrite some notes if I studied in a café, type notes if I was at my desk, hand draw mind maps, type up quizzes, scribble down some essay plans and type up my reflections. You can use a blended approach by printing out your typed notes and filing them in one physical folder.

Tips for handwritten or typed notes

- Add titles and page numbers to your notes to keep them organized.
- Use different colours and styles (bold, italic, underline) to enhance and distinguish between various elements.
- Create your own abbreviations to speed up your writing eg '>' for increase, 'w' for with, 'w/o' for without, etc.
- Scan your handwritten notes using an app like Scannable or CamScanner.
- Always back up your notes on an external hard drive and/or cloud-based service such as DropBox, OneDrive or Google Drive.

Action steps

- Identify the end use of your notes – essays or exams.
- Create lists of the note-taking location and content clues.
- Decide on a note-taking method, or a combination of a few, to test.
- Decide on handwritten, typed or blended note taking and test.

12
Essay writing

The essay creation process includes three types of activities: planning, writing and editing. A typical student likely spends 10 per cent of their time planning, 80 per cent writing and 10 per cent editing. However, I want to encourage you to try a more balanced split of 25:50:25 – because in my experience, an essay is *made* during the planning and editing phases.

Planning your essay thoroughly allows you to understand the task, so you can write a piece that *actually* answers the question. Editing enables you to strengthen each part of your essay and review your entire answer against the question and guidance.

Planning

I've found that there are two main camps that students belong to when it comes to essay-writing strategy.

Upfront planning:

- Longer planning process – time-consuming, difficult at times.
- Methodical approach to planning and writing.
- Writing and editing take less time.
- Potential to gain higher marks through closer alignment between what you've been asked to write and what you've written.

Full steam ahead:

- Minimal planning process.
- Allows for creativity and flexibility.
- 'Kitchen sink' method of writing any and all ideas.
- Longer editing process needed to ensure all points are relevant to the question/topic.
- Potential to lose marks if editing doesn't happen or is rushed.

You may immediately see yourself in one of these descriptions or you may be somewhere in between. And although it might seem like I'm going to tell you that upfront planning is best… actually, there's no right or wrong answer. Instead, it's important for you to understand your strategy and exploit it. For the 'upfront planning' crew, it takes a lot longer to actually start writing the essay but once you have, writing and editing are a lot easier. It's important for this group to make sure they know HOW to plan properly.

For the 'full steam ahead' team, you'll start writing a lot faster – but there are two possible problems. Either you'll need to spend a long time reviewing your work and cutting unnecessary words, or you're at risk of losing marks if you don't dedicate a good chunk of time to editing your work multiple times.

Ok, so I fibbed a tiny bit – I am going to advocate for the 'upfront planning' strategy. No matter your natural style, devoting time and effort to creating a great essay plan will help you achieve higher grades, as you'll come out of the planning phase with an essay outline that clearly and accurately answers the set question. Planning will also help you write clear, strong arguments, engage in critical thinking and write a powerful, give-me-all-the-marks conclusion. If you're not a natural planner, I'd encourage you to read this section and give it a go, even if the very idea fills you with dread.

Five steps to an excellent essay plan

This process is designed for essays where you are given a set question or choice of questions to answer. It's still useful for assignments where you have to come up with your own question, but for these, you can skip step three.

1 Set up your essay document

Create a new document for your next essay and save it in a sensible folder with a sensible file name that includes the necessary elements such as name, student number, module code, essay reference and version number (check your student handbook or other assessment guidance to find out what exactly you need to include).

Then, edit the header and footer to include the details your guidance sets out, such as page numbers and your name or student number. Next, look at your essay question and guidance, identify the pages and sections your essay needs, and add them in. You might need a title page, contents page and a page for your reference list or bibliography.

Setting up your document will keep your essay organized, so you can jump around and add bits to sections without creating chaos.

> **Top tip**
>
> I normally set up my essay documents as soon as I submit the previous one, even if I'm not going to start the next piece for a few weeks. Then, when you do begin writing, you won't have to start from a blank page and you'll feel motivated to continue.

2 Collect the guidance

Create a new page in your document, copy and paste the entire essay question and change its colour to make it stand out. Then, add all the guidance underneath the question: the word count, directions for answering the question, formatting guidelines, marking criteria or learning outcomes, etc. This is also a great place to record any informal guidance you get from your tutor; any snippets of advice they've given in e-mails or during class.

Having all your guidance in one place will keep you organized, refresh your memory during the writing phase, and provide an easy way to double-check that your answer is ticking all those high-grade boxes.

3 Break down the question

The single most important part of essay writing is understanding the question that's been set. You may write an absolutely brilliant essay that has your tutor on the edge of their seat as they read it, but if you haven't answered the question or you haven't met the requirements of their marking criteria, then they simply cannot give you the marks.

To understand the question, you need to understand the essay directives – the verbs or 'doing' words. To help you, here are the most common directives with an explanation for each. Use it as a reference during your essay writing to check you're answering the *right* question. You can download a printable version of this table from www.koganpage.com/return-to-study-handbook.

Table 12.1 Essay directives

Analyse	Identify and examine its key elements, their strengths and weaknesses and the relationship between them.
Assess	Decide to what extent something is useful, valuable or true. Identify strengths and weaknesses and come to a logical decision.
Compare or contrast	Identify and explain the similarities *(or differences)* between two or more concepts, ideas, theories. Decide if some are stronger or more important. You may also be expected to explain the alternative.
Compare and contrast	Identify and explain the similarities *and* differences between two or more concepts, ideas, theories. Decide if some are stronger or more important. If appropriate, make a choice and justify.
Critically assess/ critically evaluate	Gather and weigh up the evidence for and against something. Come to a final conclusion after reasoned judgement.
Define	Give the precise meaning of a term or idea. You may have to consider different definitions or interpretations and outline any issues in defining the meaning.
Describe	Identify and provide a detailed explanation of something. This could include its features or answering questions like *what*, *how* and *why*?
Discuss	Present both sides or pros and cons; elaborate and build a case for each, then come to a conclusion.
Evaluate	*Similar to critically assess/evaluate.*
Examine	Consider and investigate the key features, issues and facts of a topic. You may need to include critique and determine which ideas are the most important.
Explain	Detail the what, why, when and how of an issue. Outline and describe its key features, causes, process or timeline.
Explore	Identify and discuss different perspectives of an idea or issue. Evaluate these perspectives and form a reasoned final argument.
Illustrate	Explain your answer using examples, case studies, diagrams, evidence or statistics.
Justify	Present an argument, supported with a body of evidence. Explain decision-making process and possible objections. Include balance by considering alternative viewpoints.
Outline	Give the main points and essential details in an organized manner, omitting minor points.

(continued)

Table 12.1 (Continued)

Review	Describe and explain the main points of the subject/issue. Ensure you include critical examination and assessment, not just description.
Summarize	Condense and present the main facts, ideas, strengths and limitations. Leave out details and elaboration.

Take your essay question, identify the directives and look up their explanations in this list. Here's an example:

> Explain why collaborations spanning organization boundaries fail. Draw on the case studies in Units 3 and 4 as well as theory from other units to illustrate the issues.

DIRECTIVE 1: Explain > *Detail the what, why, when and how of an issue. Outline and describe its key features, causes, process or timeline.*

DIRECTIVE 2: Illustrate > *Explain your answer using examples, case studies, diagrams, evidence or statistics.*

Then try to pick apart the question's elements. Doing this before you start writing will help you form a coherent argument that tells a story rather than an essay that jumps around illogically. The clearer your argument, the easier it will be for your tutor to understand your ideas and award you marks.

Here's another example:

> Describe the process of rational decision making and evaluate its usefulness to managers.

The directives for this question are 'describe' and 'evaluate'. If you dive deeper, you'll find the question can be split into various sections that will need answering to write a high-grade essay.

The sections are:

- Describe the rational decision-making process.
- Evaluate its usefulness to managers:
  - reasons why it *is* useful;
  - reasons why it is *not* useful.
- Conclusion on usefulness of the process to managers.

Once you've got an idea of sections, create a new page for each in your essay document. You now have clear space to tackle each one when you get to the writing stage.

4 Sources and references

Reread the essay's question, and your guidance, and then locate the course material you're going to need as you write. List the textbooks, and specifically the chapters or pages that will be useful. Find any other relevant readings, articles or videos. If more research is needed, brainstorm some topic ideas for later.

When it's time for you to conduct research for your essays, your first step should be to get support tailored to your situation – the best research methods will differ between subjects, institutions and library systems. If you have one, go and visit your librarian and ask for their advice and tips. If not, ask your tutor or another member of faculty staff if they have a researching guide. You should be able to get advice on the different systems and tools, and tips on how to hone your searches for more accurate results.

5 Theories and concepts

Lastly, make a list of any possible theories, theorists, concepts, models, diagrams and so on that you could include in your essay. Scan the question and guidance for key words to give you ideas.

It's important that you ask for help if you have any questions during this process, or if there are parts of the task or guidance you don't fully understand. Contact your tutor for clarification or ideas if you get stuck.

This five-step planning process may take you an hour, but it will definitely be worth it. You can now move forward with a full understanding of the task you've been set, and ideas for sources and material you can explore for content.

Writing

Starting the writing process of your essay can seem daunting, so I want to give you a few more steps to complete once you've got your plan and you're ready to go.

Essay-writing kick-off

1 Decide on the ingredients

The basis of any essay is: make a point, back it up with evidence, and repeat. This means that for every point you want to make in your essay you also need some form of evidence from books, articles, websites, videos, etc.

Have a think about the other ingredients needed for your essay. If your question asks you to illustrate your argument using examples, then as well as your own points and theory you'll also need points from some relevant examples. Another essay may ask you to comment on your learning, so reflections will be another ingredient for your essay. Other ingredients could be strengths, weaknesses or recommendations.

Make a list of your ingredients and refer back to it throughout your writing process to ensure you include each of them the right amount. Writing entire sections that don't include all the ingredients will make for weaker writing.

2 Brainstorm your points

Go through your notes, and all the material you identified as relevant for your essay, and start combing for relevant points. Use your set up essay document and add these useful points to the relevant pages or sections to start building a collection of possible material for your answer.

If you've got research to conduct, now's the time to do it. Find and read the articles, highlight the relevant points, and add them to your collection.

3 Piece together a draft

Take your brainstorm and start piecing together your draft. Find points that are relevant to each other and try and form them into coherent arguments, using your ingredients list as a reminder for the types of sentences you need to include.

Signposts and transitions

It's important to bring your writing back to the question or topic often to show the reader (your tutor) not only that you understand your work, but also that you are in control of your essay's journey. You can use a writing tool called 'signposting' to link your argument back to the aim of the essay.

Signposts are words or phrases that indicate the direction of your essay and highlight key points you're making and conclusions you're drawing. They keep the reader engaged and make it blatantly clear how you're answering the question – and that you deserve some marks!

Here are some examples of signposts you can use in your writing.

- 'Having discussed the strengths of Theory X, its limitations will now be outlined.'
- 'A further argument for the usefulness of Theory Y is…'
- 'A counter argument to Smith's claims is…'

- 'To further understand the importance of Z…'
- 'Figure 2.0 demonstrates how Company A exhibits [insert reference related to the question].'

As you wrap up each argument or point, get in the habit of adding a punchy concluding signpost sentence which refers back to the question and explains how your argument answers part of it, eg 'X demonstrates that [insert reference related to the question]'.

Transitions are linking words and phrases that work together with signposts to progress your writing and connect one point to another. Without transitions, your essay would read as a series of unrelated statements – which we don't want. You're probably already using some of these words without realizing their full power, so here are some examples to include in your next essay.

To indicate similarity in your points:

- Additionally, …
- Furthermore, …
- Similarly, …
- Also, …
- Likewise, …

To indicate contrast in your points:

- Nevertheless, …
- Alternatively, …
- Conversely, …
- Yet, …

To exemplify a point:

- For example, …
- To illustrate, …
- For instance, …

To indicate effect or consequence:

- Thus, …
- Therefore, …
- As a result, …
- Consequently, …

Academic writing

Your tutor has a lot of essays to read and mark. When they get to your essay in the pile and read through it, how do you want them to feel? Do you want them to sigh, rub their throbbing temple and force themselves to reread your unclear writing? Or do you want them to smile at your lovely writing that walks them round your clear ideas?

A well-written, clear essay makes it easier for your tired, busy tutor to understand the flow of your ideas and award you the marks your hard work deserves. Academic writing is expected at university or college, but it can be tricky if you've never been taught how to write clearly and professionally. Have no fear, though, because we're going to look at some tips you can use in your next essay.

1 Do not use clichés, colloquialisms or contractions

While I can use contractions and informality in this book and in my blog posts, in academic writing they're a no-no, so as to preserve objectivity and neutrality. Therefore, make sure you stay away from contractions such as 'don't', 'can't', 'couldn't', and use their full versions instead.

Similarly, you want your academic writing to be clear and formal – so avoid using text-speak or colloquialisms like 'kinda', 'ain't' or 'gonna', or clichés such as 'at the end of the day' or 'only time will tell'.

2 Back up all your points

The common formula for an essay is to make a point, then back this up with evidence and a reference. The evidence might come from course theory, research, an example or case study. Using examples and theory strengthens your claims, demonstrates you understand and can apply the material, and can gain you more marks. *Always* include a reference if you've taken your point from a source (and not your own head) – check your course guidance for information on plagiarism and the preferred referencing style to find out how you should do this.

3 Be objective

In academic writing you must demonstrate objectivity – an unbiased, neutral perspective. Unless an essay asks for your opinion, do not express judgement on the material. Instead, you need to find evidence to support your arguments and your conclusions should be drawn from this evidence, not your own viewpoints. This seems a little cold… but it's objectivity that allows for trusted, useful research.

If you're writing an essay where you have to decide on one side of an argument, your decision in the conclusion should not come as a surprise to the reader (your tutor). It's your unbiased, objective analysis of the different perspectives and the evidence that supports them that forms your conclusion.

4 Use the correct point of view

Most academic writing requires the use of the third-person point of view, using the pronouns 'he' and 'she', rather than first-person 'I'. Objective academic writing is made up of arguments built from unbiased analysis of evidence. This means first person is inappropriate here. Instead of saying, 'I believe', you should say, 'The evidence suggests'. Instead of saying, 'In this essay I will analyse…', you should say, 'This essay will analyse…'.

However, some essays will require first person and the use of 'I' if they include self-reflection or your own research. Before starting each essay, double-check (with your tutor or the guidance) what point of view you should use.

5 Avoid very long sentences

Remember the phrase *one idea, one sentence*, and try to apply the principle in your writing. Short sentences like this one can add impact. And long sentences like this one are great for adding necessary details and analysis, but if you use too many, and make them too complex (uh-oh), then the reader can become confused, and by the time they reach the end of the sentence they can't remember what they read at the beginning – which is bad luck for you. And breathe…

Read your essay out loud and edit any sentences that are too long for you to read comfortably. Scan through for sentences where you've switched points and started talking about another idea. I normally copy the offending sentence and paste it into some blank space. Play around with the order and remove some words until you've improved the clarity.

Start and end with a bang

Your essay's introduction is like a concert's opening. It sets the tone for the rest of the evening and gets the audience excited for what's to come. I've come up with a simple formula that you can use as a base for a great introduction:

> **Sexy statement + version of the essay question + structure outline**

Kick off your introduction with a few sentences introducing the essay topic, giving necessary background information and explaining the key concept. You might start with a powerful quotation to grab the reader's attention.

Next, restate the essay question, ie, 'This essay aims to investigate/analyse [version of essay question]. Then, use a few sentences to outline how you will answer the essay, the sources you will use or the key concepts you will analyse.

I use this formula as a starting point in my own essays, and advise my clients to use it too, because it's pretty simple to write these three components. However, you'll need to check your essay guidance to see if there are any additional ingredients you should include, or specific rules about the contents or length of an introduction.

An essay's conclusion is normally the rushed few hundred words you complete just before submission. But they *could* be a powerful way to sign off your essay and prove its value to the reader. Dancing out of a music concert still singing that final number is an amazing feeling that stays with you – and it's the same for your essay. Your essay's conclusion needs to end your piece with a bang and cement the idea that the experience was worth the audience's time. Throughout, you've laid down threads of arguments which your conclusion must draw together.

Unfortunately, I don't have a one-size-fits-all formula for a great conclusion, but I do have some tips for you:

- Summarize the key findings – but try to go one step further and synthesize them. This means not just repeating your points but showing your reader what new insight comes from their combination.
- General advice says not to introduce new material into a conclusion, but you could try and find an interesting insight or quotation if it fits with your evidence.
- Ask yourself the question, 'so what?' to engage your critical thinking and help you come up with material for your conclusion. Go through your essay and after each argument, ask yourself, 'so what?' Dig deeper into what you've written and explain why it matters. What are you trying to say? What does this point add to your answer? What conclusions can you draw? For example, you might have thought of some circumstances where a model would not apply in practice. You could note down, 'Because there are numerous situations where Model X does not apply, it can be argued this model is limited.' Use this list to help you form the points for your conclusion.

- You could comment on the broader context around your essay topic, or make recommendations for action, solutions or questions for further study.
- Include a restatement of the essay question, similar to the introduction, but this time embed it in a sentence that demonstrates how your essay answers or contributes to the question and why.

Critical thinking

Critical thinking. Two words that evoke fear in a lot of students. Tutors bang on about it and assignments often require you demonstrate it if you want to achieve the high marks. But it doesn't have to be that scary! In fact, probably without realizing it, you engage in critical thinking *all the time*.

When you decide to buy a new car, for example, you hunt for information to help you make a decision. You take advice from car salespeople and reviews from friends, the internet and magazines and you determine their value. You may detect bias in the Ford salesperson's advice when they try to persuade you not to buy a Volkswagen from the dealership up the road. You make judgements on some of the reviews you read, and guess that some of them are sponsored. You weigh up the strengths and weaknesses of your options before making a reasoned decision.

This is critical thinking – the process of evaluating and critiquing information to make judgements on its value. Students with critical thinking skills can:

- weigh up different sides of an argument and draw logical conclusions;
- compare and contrast ideas;
- defend arguments against bias and a lack of evidence;
- determine the strengths and weaknesses of ideas;
- identify the links between information;
- make judgements on the value of a claim based on its evidence;
- form stronger arguments;
- *achieve higher grades* (the most important benefit, I know!)

If you've ever had assignment feedback like the examples below, then improving your critical thinking skills will help you increase your grades in future:

- 'Too much description and not enough analysis.'
- 'You made some illogical assumptions.'

- 'You started well but didn't dig deep enough.'
- 'So what? What does your argument show?'
- 'You've included good points, but you need to evaluate the material.'

How to flex your critical thinking muscles

Here are some questions to ask yourself when writing your essays to develop your skills as a critical thinker. Ask them of the evidence you're using – but also ask them of your own writing.

Questions of analysis

- **Are the evidence and material recent?** Are there environmental changes that have made the information less relevant or accurate? Check with your tutor if you're not sure.
- **Who is the author?** An author's background influences their research and can affect the usefulness of their material in other contexts. Be sure to question an author's findings rather than accept their opinions as fact.
- **Are there any issues with the methodology?** Analyse studies you're using to check for issues with sample sizes, representation, bias, assumptions and variables.
- **Can you spot any gaps?** Do you have any unanswered questions, or have you left any holes in your own work?
- **What assumptions have been made?** Be sure to identify and question the assumptions you make in your writing, and that others make in the material you're studying. Are any incorrect, illogical or biased?

Questions of application

- **What problems does the material solve or explain?** What are the concept's strengths and how can the information be applied to answer your essay question?
- **Are there situations where the concepts don't work or aren't as useful?** For example, for a business essay, does the concept apply to both young and old companies, large and small, bureaucratic and innovative, public and private sector, profit or non-profit, companies all over the world or just those in specific countries?

- **Does the argument flow?** Make sure your essay lays out its points in a clear, sensible order so the arguments build and lead to a logical conclusion.

Questions of evaluation

- **Have all sides of the argument been considered?** Analyse your evidence to determine if various perspectives have been acknowledged, explained or considered. Do the same for your own writing.
- **Are the conclusions accurate and logical?** Check the conclusions of the evidence and your own material for logic. They should make sense from the evidence provided and not be a surprise for the reader.

Editing

Editing may seem like a nice-to-have rather than a must-have when you're writing an essay. I know you're tired and you just wanna hit that submit button. You've given it a quick read-through, that's enough, right?

Wrong. Making time to edit your essay properly *will* pay off, because a thorough proofread could gain you 10 to 15 per cent more marks – an entire grade boundary in a lot of courses.

Spelling mistakes, grammatical errors, incomplete sentences, odd punctuation, disrupted flow of sentences – all of this can mask the great nuggets of literary gold you've whooped your butt to write.

A well-written, proofread essay will demonstrate clearly to your tutor that you are the bee's knees – that you understand the course materials *and* the essay question. Make time to proofread, and your tutor will find it easier to award you marks.

Top tips for editing your essay

1 Act, reflect. Act, reflect

Author Steven Pressfield (2011) explains in his book *Do the Work* that the writing process consists of two stages: action and reflection. In essay terms, this means writing and editing. He explains that we should focus on one at a time. First we write, then we proofread, then we write again – the two activities should never be bundled together.

Trying to write your essay *and* worry about the flow and overall structure at the same time will cripple your creativity and start sowing those charming seeds of I-can't-do-this doubt into your mind. I had a moment of this chaos myself writing this book. I tried to act and reflect, write and proofread all at the same time and it was con.fus.ing. In fact, my publisher had to repeat my own words back to me and tell me to stop multitasking!

So, I get it. As you're writing, if you notice glaring, super-quick-to-fix issues then, sure, go ahead and fix them. But, ultimately, you should aim to write without fear. This is one of the reasons I love an essay plan; you've already done some of the hard work to get clear on your direction, which leaves you free in the writing stage to focus just on the writing, safe in the knowledge you can realign any detours from the path during editing.

2 Take a break

Your brain is going to feel like a soggy, fried mushroom that's been run over by an SUV when you finish writing. And a sautéed noggin is not the best tool for editing – so step *away* from your work for a few hours (or even a few days if you have time) and come back to it with a fresh brain and fresh eyes.

3 Print to proofread

If you can access a printer, always print your essay a few times during the editing process. A lot of people (me included) find it easier to notice mistakes on printed paper than on screens. And you can mark up a printed essay easily by crossing parts out, drawing arrows and adding other points in the margins. Take this annotated sheet and make the amendments to your digital copy.

4 Go back to the question and guidance

The guidance you're given alongside your essay question is important, so make sure you don't simply glance at it a few times. Use it *throughout* as your roadmap to meeting all the criteria for a high grade.

During the editing process, keep a copy of the question and guidance nearby so you can check that you've completed or met the criteria for every. single. part – tick 'em off as you go.

5 Proofread for just one element

It's going to be pretty overwhelming if you try to scan your essay for grammatical errors, weak sentence structure, repeated words, incorrect references… all at the same time. Instead, proofread with just one element in mind. Yes, this does mean editing won't be a one-and-done job, but you bought this book because you're serious, right?

Choose an element to review, such as referencing, and proofread just for that. Then choose another element – I promise you it'll be worth it.

See the box for a checklist you can use for all your future essays. You can download an online version from www.koganpage.com/return-to-study-handbook.

> **Editing checklist**
>
> Review spellcheck (with the correct proofing language set) ☐
> Check proper names are correct and capitalization of terms and names is consistent ☐
> Check acronyms are correct (write out an acronym in full the first time with the acronym in brackets and thereafter just use the acronym, eg National Aeronautics and Space Administration (NASA) and then just NASA) ☐
> Check all figures and statistics ☐
> Check every point is backed up by evidence/theory/examples ☐
> Check formatting of full and in-text references and ensure none are forgotten ☐
> Check each section links back to the question ☐
> Check that overall formatting is consistent with your course guidance/style guide ☐
> Use a thesaurus to replace overly repeated words (but double-check for the same meaning) ☐
> Read through and tick off every point of the question and guidance your essay meets ☐
> Read aloud to check for sentence flow and punctuation ☐
> Check you've included signposts and transition words to link ideas and sections ☐
> Take a break before the final edits ☐

Essay Writing

Read aloud to check for errors or get Microsoft Word to read ☐
your essay to you! (The settings differ by operating system.
In Word for PCs, find the Quick Access Toolbar at the top
of the page, select More Commands, find Speak, then hit Add to add
it to your toolbar. On a Mac the option is Read Aloud but first
go to System Preferences > Accessibility > Speech to set this up)

Action steps

- Work out whether you're an Upfront Planner or a Full Steam Ahead-er. If you're the former, allocate more time for planning and if you're the latter, allocate more time for editing.
- When you have an essay to work on:
    - Set up your essay document and collect the guidance.
    - Break down your essay question.
    - Collect your sources, references and relevant points.
    - Follow the Essay-Writing Kick-off process to write your first draft.
    - Use the guidance/formula for an effective introduction and conclusion.
    - Follow the academic writing tips.
    - Use the critical thinking questions to improve your work.
    - Use the editing checklist to review your work.

Part Five
Exam preparation

13
Exam revision

Exams are scary for a lot of students. Maybe it's the stress of trying to remember everything you've learned, or perhaps you have negative memories of past exams.

But exams are necessary, ultimately, so your university or college can get a clear picture of your level of knowledge and understanding of the course material, and assign the correct grade to you. During your exam revision, you'll notice where you have knowledge gaps, which gives you the opportunity to fill them. Also, the process of searching your memory and retrieving relevant material will strengthen your ability to recall it – which will help you achieve a high grade in your exam.

> **Exam vs essay**
>
> You may be like me in that you'd much prefer to write an essay than take an exam. You have time to plan and refine an essay whereas an exam is passed or failed in such a short window of time. However, it's not all doom and gloom! Exams do have some advantages over essays. For most courses, examiners are more lenient than tutors about spelling mistakes, grammatical errors and left out details. Your answers are expected to be less detailed than an unexamined essay on the same subject. Also, a module with an exam at the end may be less stressful long-term than a module with lots of regular assignments instead.

Let's look at some key strategies you need to be able to step into that exam hall feeling confident that you've prepared in the best way you can.

Exam investigation

Your exam's format, topics and instructions should never surprise you on the day. You don't want to turn over your paper and realize you've revised the wrong things or not practised the right type of questions. For one of my maths exams at school I got to the exam and realized the key formulas were not included in the formula book and I hadn't memorized them – that was *not* a fun exam!

As soon as you're told about your exam, take the chance to do some investigation so you can be as prepared as possible. Take a piece of paper and answer the following questions:

- When is your exam? Date and time.
- Where will it be?
- How long is it?
- What weighting does it have towards your final module/year grade?
- What grade do you need to pass?
- What grade do you *want*?
- If you have multiple exams, which one is the most important to your final grade?
- Do you have other important assignments close to your exam? If so, which is the most important?
- What type of exam is it?
- What topics will the exam cover?

Let's dive deeper into those last two questions now.

Different types of written exam

Written exams can be categorized in three different ways: the style of questions, your prior knowledge of the questions, and the resources allowed in the exam. Identify your type of exam from these categories.

Style of questions

Multiple choice This is an exam where you have to recognize and select the correct answer(s) from a number of options.

Advantages:

- The correct answer *is* there.
- The questions are often simpler (not requiring higher-level, critical thinking skills).

- Each question has a lower mark, so one incorrect question will have a lower impact on your final grade.

Disadvantage: A broad range of knowledge is needed to be able to distinguish between similar, incorrect answers.

Short-answer questions This is an exam where the questions require an answer ranging from 100–700 words with a focus on describing, explaining, applying or analysing the material.

Advantages:

- You won't be expected to know everything about each topic.
- You can use the number of marks per question to gauge the detail and length of your answer – for example, a five-mark question will normally require five points or details.

Disadvantage: You need to revise a wide range of topics *and* pay attention to your formatting *and* remember to present your answer logically.

Essay-based/long-answer questions This is an exam made up of a smaller number of questions requiring longer, essay-style answers.

Advantages:

- Patterns may emerge over years of exams, so you can anticipate possible questions or topics.
- You won't be expected to produce an answer as detailed as a normal, unexamined essay.

Disadvantages:

- You risk losing a lot of marks if you're unsure on a question or can't remember the topics.
- You need a deep understanding of the material to build a coherent argument with critical analysis.

Prior knowledge of the questions

Unseen An unseen exam is where you do not know what the questions will be before you turn over the paper. However, you should always know the range of material the exam *could* cover. This is the format for most written exams.

Advantage: With solid revision you should be able to tackle whatever questions come up.

Disadvantages:

- These exams can be more stressful.
- Incomplete or ineffective revision could leave you struggling on some of the questions.

Seen A seen exam is one where you are told in advance either the specific topics that will be tested, or even the exact questions, so you can plan your answers in advance. When I first heard of this type of exam, I wondered why they call it an exam and not an essay. For some subjects, a clearer understanding of a student's abilities and knowledge can be achieved through essays that allow time for exploration, research and analysis. To fight the fact that it's pretty easy to cheat in essays, some universities and colleges compromise by setting a seen exam which gives students time to prepare in advance, but they have to write their answers in exam conditions.

Advantages:

- Less stress and anxiety.
- You can target your revision to just the concepts you'll need.

Disadvantages:

- You will still need a deep understanding of the relevant material.
- You'll need to master essay-writing techniques.
- You'll need to memorize your prepared answers.

Allowed resources

Closed book A closed book exam is where you have no resources with you during the exam and must rely on your memorization of the material.

Advantage: *Most* universities or colleges won't expect you to include every single detail to get a high grade.

Disadvantage: Your success relies greatly on your ability to recall the course material. If you struggle to memorize concepts, don't worry – we'll look at how to remember what you've learned in a moment.

Open book An open book exam is where you're allowed to bring some or all of the course materials in with you. This will differ between institutions – you may be allowed to bring in your notes and/or your annotated textbooks.

Advantage: You have your material in front of you so you don't need to panic that you'll forget a key detail from your notes.

Disadvantages:

- Your notes need to be organized so you can find stuff quickly.
- Your understanding of the material needs to be deeper, because your questions will require higher-level thinking such as application, analysis and evaluation.

Now you know the types of exams, identify the three characteristics of your exam. For example, many of my university exams were closed book, unseen and essay-based questions. Maybe yours is open book, unseen and multiple-choice questions. Later in the chapter, we'll look at some specific tips and strategies for your exam type.

Exam content

Identify the range of topics your exam could cover. Could anything from your module or year come up, or is the exam focused on specific topics? You can find this out by asking your tutor, talking to your university or college, or looking in your module handbook.

Once you know what *might* come up, try creating an exam concept mind map. Take a blank piece of paper and write your exam title in the centre. Then, using the information you discovered, start adding the topics and concepts you need to revise around the outside. Use your textbooks and notes to help you with this – get specific, and list out individual theories, concepts and models.

This will become your go-to resource throughout your revision. Use it to check your progress and ensure you haven't missed out any key topics.

Key exam principles

There are two key things you need to understand and implement for successful exam revision and higher grades.

Principle #1 – active learning

Passive learning is 'traditional' classroom teaching, where the student receives information from their tutor, or reads and internalizes information from a textbook. It doesn't require a particularly high level of engagement, and includes techniques like taking notes, rewriting notes or reading through revision notes or flashcards. Some passivity is necessary to start the learning and connection process, but if you only stick with passive learning, you'll only ever get surface-level learning, stopping at understanding the broad, initial parts of a concept.

Active learning is a different approach. It's centred around engagement, meaning that you take control of your own learning. It takes *effort*; you can't sit in class daydreaming, you have to participate! You can't accept everything you read and simply try to memorize it, you have to question it and understand it. Active learning includes testing your knowledge, problem solving, applying a concept to real life, questioning concepts, drawing conclusions and synthesizing ideas (coming up with your own, new ideas).

Imagine this: you have a few days until a big exam and you've sat down for some revision. You know you should probably test yourself with a practice paper... but that's *hard*... so instead, you decide to read through your revision notes again. Great! This feels *a lot* easier. You recognize the ideas so, fingers crossed, you'll remember everything in the exam! Cut to a few days later – you're partway through your exam and you feel like walking out. You're trying to remember key concepts, but you can only remember snippets of details. You thought the information was in your head – but it's not!

This is because *recognition is an illusion of competence*. Rereading your notes can trick you into thinking you know the material because the words feel familiar to you. As you skim through them, you think to yourself, 'I know this.' But in the exam, you're probably not going to have your notes with you (unless it's an open book exam). Recalling a concept, instead of recognizing it when it's in front of you, is a much harder process; you don't have your material in front of you as a prompt. To be able to *recall* a concept, you need a deep understanding of it... which is unlikely to happen simply through passive learning.

Taking notes and condensing them down to summaries are fairly passive activities, although they are useful at the beginning of your revision. Simply rereading your notes isn't going to cut it though, so it's time to embrace active learning.

Active learning *is* uncomfortable. You're probably going to hate it at times because it places what you do and don't know right in front of your face. If you don't get something, you're not going to be able to bury your head in the sand and forget about it. Active learning is hard… but it's going to help you *so* much. It will allow you to deepen your understanding and retain the material you need for your exams. You'll be able to immediately spot the areas where you are less confident, so you know where to focus your studying attention… and increase your grades.

Here's a list of active revision techniques for you to try out during revision for your next exam:

- test yourself with flashcards and quizzes;
- practise with exam questions and papers;
- create mind maps and posters *and* test yourself with them;
- find links between ideas;
- apply an idea to a real-life situation;
- discuss ideas with a friend;
- understand a formula's underlying principles (for mathematical or scientific subjects).

Principle #2 – spaced repetition

It's not enough to reread your notes for a module or make a few flashcards and read them once or twice. Effective revision that's going to help you achieve a high grade requires you to test your knowledge of a concept *multiple times*.

The forgetting curve describes the phenomenon of the decline of recall in human memory. The second you learn a concept, your retention is 100 per cent, but the information will quickly disappear from your brain over the next few days – which explains why we often can't remember what we studied yesterday or last week. This was researched and named by Hermann Ebbinghaus in his 1885 work, *Über das Gedchtnis*; see Wozniak (1999).

Spaced repetition is a method that builds on Ebbinghaus' work, developed by Piotr Woźniak (2018). Simply put, spaced repetition is the process of testing your knowledge of a concept *multiple times* in order to improve your retention of that concept *over time*. It works like this: when you review a concept, your retention goes back up to 100 per cent, as it's fresh in your brain – just like that initial point on the forgetting curve. However, the

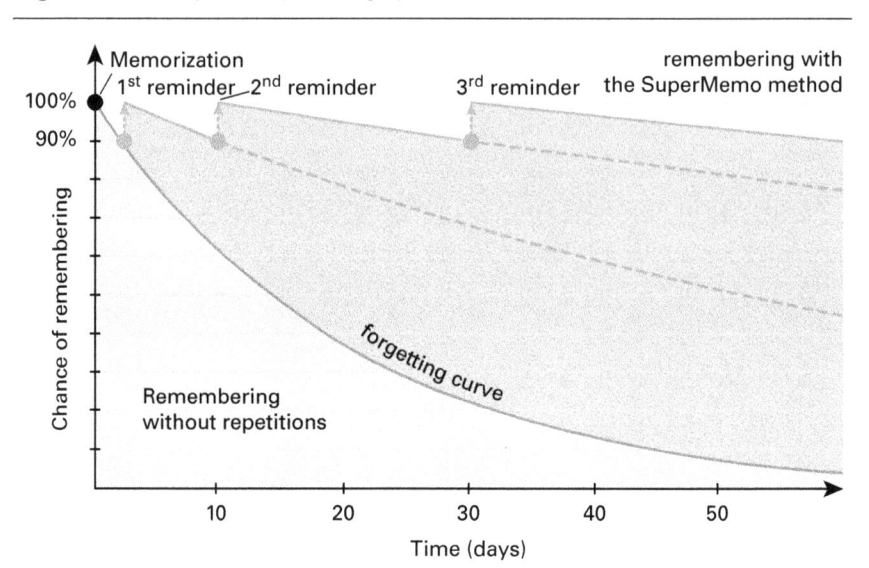

Figure 13.1 Spaced repetition graph

second time you take in the same information, the downwards, 'forgetting' part of the curve is different. The decrease is a lot shallower – because you've strengthened the memory. This means that you will be able to recall the information for longer. With each review your memory strengthens and the curve continues to decrease.

The time between each retest is dependent on how well you know the concept – because there's no point going over and over the stuff you really know, leaving the confusing stuff untested. You should retest more often on the concepts you know the least, and less often on the concepts you know well. Essentially, you need to review your material *multiple times* to increase the amount you will be able to recall in an exam.

Active revision techniques

Flashcards

Flashcards are a brilliant, active revision method for learning the relationship between two pieces of information – either a question and answer, or a term and definition. If created correctly, and used multiple times, you will *vastly* increase the amount of material you can recall in your exams. You can use physical flashcards, making them yourself using index cards, or there are some great resources out there for digital flashcards. Personally, I like the SuperMemo software – developed by Woźniak (the guy from the last section who developed the concept of spaced repetition). You can get it as a web app, or as an iOS, Android, or Windows app, and there are both paid and free versions.

A lot of students (past Chloe included) list bullet points onto flashcards then carry them around and reread them. But, as you now know, rereading your notes is a passive learning technique – so we need to make our flashcards active. Here are my best tips for creating fantastic flashcards.

1 **One idea, one card.** On the front of the card write a key term or question, and on the back of the card write the definition or answer. That's it – no more bulleted lists. Your brain will struggle to recall multiple pieces of information, so keep each flashcard to one idea and split longer, complex questions into smaller pieces. You'll end up with a lot of flashcards, but they'll be *so* much more effective.

2 **Don't use other people's flashcards.** Creating your own flashcards, ideally by rewriting the concepts into your own words, starts off the process of understanding the material. You then strengthen that understanding through testing.

3 **Use images *and* words.** Developmental biologist and memory expert, John Medina, outlines the Pictorial Superiority Effect in his book *Brain Rules* (Medina, 2008). He explains that our brains actually see words as lots of tiny images that have to be processed – which means pictures beat text! In his research, Medina discovered that, after three days, a person is likely to remember around 10 per cent of information presented as text. If a picture is added to the text, then a person is likely to remember *65 per cent* of the information. Images are easier to remember because they take less processing for the brain.

Try to add pictures to your flashcards and other revision material. You may not think pictures are relevant to your study material, but I challenge you to have a go. For authors or people, you could draw a face or stick figure. For places, you could draw a quick map or any item that belongs to that place, eg a croissant for France. For figures you could draw a graph, and for dates, sequences and processes you could draw a timeline or flowchart. Simple sketches will improve your brain's encoding of the material (Medina, 2008) so it sticks in your brain and you're more likely to recall it in an exam.

4 **Use cloze tests.** In 1953, Wilson L Taylor from the University of Illinois created the cloze deletion test where words are removed from a piece of text and the participant is asked to replace those missing words (Taylor, 1953). For example, a participant would read the words 'Mount Everest rises to ... metres above sea level' and would fill this in with the words '8,848m'.

   Cloze deletion tests are great for mixing up your learning and can help to place more difficult concepts or terms within a familiar context.

5 **Use mnemonic devices.** Mnemonics are memory devices that help you recall larger pieces of information. You were probably taught a few in school. For example, a mnemonic to remember the order of colours in the rainbow is, **R**ichard **O**f **Y**ork **G**ave **B**attle **I**n **V**ain (red, orange, yellow, green, blue, indigo, violet). A different type I learned during mathematics was for remembering trigonometric functions. **SOH-CAH-TOA** stood for **s**ine = **o**pposite/**h**ypotenuse, **c**osine = **a**djacent/**h**ypotenuse and **t**angent = **o**pposite/**a**djacent.

   Mnemonics, like using pictures, improves the encoding of information which, in turn, improves your ability to recall the material to which it is linked. If you're struggling to understand a concept, see if you can create a mnemonic out of its letters, or create a rhyme or song with it.

6 **Shuffle your cards.** Always shuffle your cards each time you go through them. You know how when you hear an album a lot you learn what the next song will be? You don't want that to happen with your flashcards – you don't want your memory of a concept to be reliant on the concept before it, in case it doesn't happen in the same order in the exam. So mix 'em up!

7 **Make them early.** Create your cards as early as possible, to increase the time you have to fit in lots of tests. I achieved my highest exam grade at university when I carved some time out of my schedule each month to make flashcards for those weeks' material.

8 **Test yourself out loud.** If you test yourself in your head, then it's easy to flip the card over, read the answer and think, 'Oh yeah, that's kinda what I said!' Say your answer out loud before you turn it over, if you can, because this commits you to your answer and you'll be able to more accurately place it in the right spaced repetition group depending on your understanding.

9 **Use spaced repetition**. After the first time you've tested your knowledge of each flashcard, place them into one of three piles:
- I have no clue about this.
- I'm not too sure about this.
- I really know this.

Retest the flashcards that you don't know sooner and more often than the flashcards you do know.

Let's say you give yourself a week to revise one section of course material. On the first day, revise all the flashcards and group them into your three piles. On the second day, revise the flashcards in the 'I have no clue about this' pile. On the fourth day, revise the flashcards you were more confident with in the 'I'm not too sure about this' pile *and* the flashcards from the first group. On the seventh day, revise all the flashcards from all three piles. This method can take some getting used to, but it works!

Quizzes

Quizzes are similar to flashcards and can be a useful addition to your revision toolkit when you want to revise more complex questions.

Go through your study materials and start creating a list of quiz questions covering key concepts. Great places to find quiz content are: your notes; key points on class slides or handouts; learning outcomes or module aims; introduction, summaries and conclusions of chapters.

The simpler questions you could turn into flashcards – but the longer ones you can turn into quizzes, grouped together into chapters or sections of your course.

An example of a short question that's suitable for a flashcard would be:

Q: Who created the five-step ice-cream-selling system?

A: Martin Smith.

An example of a longer question that's more suitable for a quiz would be:

Q: What are two criticisms of Smith's five-step ice-cream-selling system?

A: It is only suitable for ice-cream shops and not vans because it requires more equipment; it can be argued that it is outdated as it doesn't take into consideration the power of social media in increasing ice-cream sales.

I hope you're proud of me for critically analysing a totally fictional ice-cream-selling concept!

On a logistical note, I've always typed my quizzes; I find it's a lot quicker. Here's my approach: create one document where you write out the questions and answers. Then duplicate this document and remove the answers so you just have the questions. Obviously, double-check your answers for clarity and accuracy – you don't want to revise an incorrect answer! It's also a good idea to number them so you can refer back easily.

Incorporate spaced repetition into your quiz practice by noting down the question numbers based on your level of confidence:

1 I have no clue about this.

2 I'm not too sure about this.

3 I really know this.

Test yourself in intervals, making sure to practise the questions you don't know more often than the ones you are confident with.

Practice exam papers

When I took my first maths exam in sixth form the questions completely stumped me. I knew how to do some of the calculations but the questions were worded in a way I'd never seen before, and I didn't even know how to *start* them. I hadn't practised with sample papers… and I failed the exam.

It's important to include testing yourself with past papers in your revision so that you can: get used to the style of questions; practise going into the required level of detail; and practise writing good answers in the time limit.

When testing yourself with exam papers, practise answering questions without a time limit first and then try again with the time limit you'll have in your exam. Practise answering questions with the help of all your textbooks and notes, and then with only the resources you're allowed in your exam (which may be nothing). Essentially, try to work your way up to answering questions in full exam conditions.

For some subjects, past papers may show that certain topics are repeated every few years. Even though you can't predict the questions that will come up (unless it's a seen exam), you can be a little bit savvy and plan your revision to include the topics and concepts that come up the most.

> **Top tip**
>
> Move on to practising with past papers once you've tested your knowledge of each concept at least once using flashcards or quizzes.

Specific techniques for different exam types

While the core principles of effective revision – active learning and spaced repetition – apply for all exam types, there are some specific tips and strategies that will help you excel in your specific exam type.

Multiple-choice questions

- Aim for understanding (not memorization) as concepts may be worded differently in your exam.
- Pay attention to similarities, differences and links between ideas, to help you rule out wrong answers and identify possible right answers.
- When practising with test papers, try to think of your answer before you see the options.

Short-answer questions

- Make sure you understand the meaning of different question words (directives) eg describe, explain, outline, apply, etc.
- For mathematical or scientific subjects, get used to showing your workings; these often gain you marks in exams.

Essay-based/long-answer questions

- Again, ensure you understand the question directives, especially those at a higher level such as evaluate, justify, and compare and contrast.
- Master your essay-writing skills: objectivity; clear, evidenced arguments; introduction; conclusion, etc.

- Practise creating simple essay plans of the key points you want to make. You could create a bulleted list, flowchart or mind map.
- Create skeleton answers from past papers which include the points, concepts, examples and analysis that you would want to include for a great answer. Creating these during your revision will develop your ability to break down a question and outline a structure quickly – skills you'll need in your exam.

Unseen

- Ensure you know the range of material your exam could cover.
- Focus on the full spectrum of revision techniques: mindmaps, flashcards, quizzes and past papers.

Seen

- Get clear on all the material related to your exam questions and focus your revision on understanding these.
- Develop your essay-writing skills: understanding directives, creating essay plans, building coherent arguments and writing outlines.
- For each exam question you want to have prepared: a plan/outline; full essay; summary of points; any examples or applied diagrams.
- Practise writing out your complete answer by hand and within the time limit, to check you can finish it.
- Turn your answer into a presentation for you to revise. Create headings and add colour and images to help you recall your points. Print this presentation out and test yourself on the elements like you would with flashcards or quizzes. Number your slides and practise recalling the headings. When you get into your exam, write down your numbered list of slides with the headings and then use this as your plan to follow.

Closed book

- Always use active revision techniques because recall and understanding are key.
- Again, improve the encoding of your revision material with pictures and mnemonics.

Open book

- Identify the material you're allowed to bring into your exam and the rules on annotation.
- If you're allowed your textbook: underline and highlight key points; add your own critical thinking to the margins; and mark key pages using different-coloured sticky notes to help you find information quickly.
- If you're allowed to bring in your notes: make them clear and legible; summarize, don't copy; number your pages; create a contents list and other lists such as key dates, terms, authors, formulas, etc.

Advice for multiple exams

Now some of you may have to revise for more than one exam at once – sometimes life likes to throw *all* the stress at you at once! I had a period during my university study where I had two completely separate business exams and six maths exams – all while working full-time and trying to complete essays for my other modules. So I know what it feels like to be utterly overwhelmed. But I got through it, and you will too – here's my best advice.

Prioritize

Complete the exam investigation and identify the importance of each of your exams to your final grades. This will help you determine how much time you should devote to them.

Schedule

Add your exam dates to your calendar so you can plan your days in the run-up to your first exam and between that and your next exam(s). Try to clear as much space as possible in that busy time in the middle of your exams by rearranging any appointments or events that can be moved.

Decide when you'll study what

Instead of telling yourself you'll revise for four hours on Sunday, identify what subjects you are going to study that day.

If you decide to revise for more than one exam on the same day, make sure you take a break between them – otherwise your brain will get confused. Put away one set of study materials, clear your desk, go for a walk and then set up for your next subject.

Identify any exam overlap

During exam investigation, identify if there's any overlap between material you'll need to revise for each exam. Obviously, there won't be for completely different subjects – but in maths, for example, exams often build upon your previous knowledge, so some concepts will come up in multiple exams.

Keep your revision materials separate

When you're studying for multiple exams, organization becomes even more important. You don't want to waste time hunting around for material or start revising a concept for the wrong exam!

Use separate folders for different subjects and mark your notes and revision material to make it easier to identify them.

The three core revision activities

Now you've learned the science behind great revision, and the most effective revision techniques for *your* exam – it's now time to plan and structure your revision.

Figure 13.2 Three core revision activities

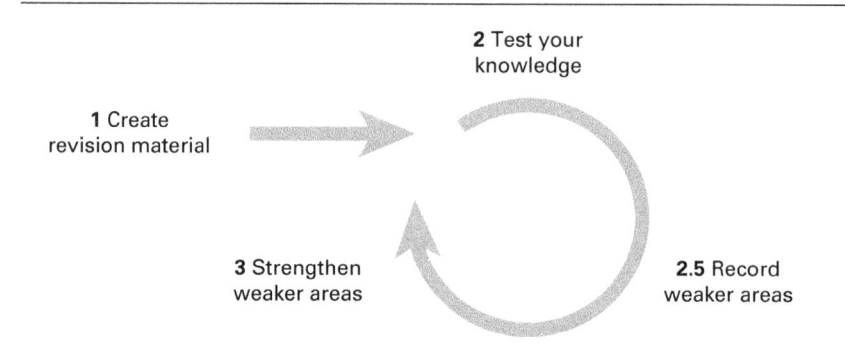

1 Create revision material

2 Test your knowledge

2.5 Record weaker areas

3 Strengthen weaker areas

There are three core revision activities you need to complete in preparation for your exam: create revision material, test your knowledge, and strengthen weaker areas.

1 Create revision material

If you haven't already got them, your next revision task (after completing your exam investigation) is to create great notes, covering the topics that could come up in the exam. This is an act of revision in itself, because summarising the material in your own words improves your understanding of the concepts.

Next, create all your other revision material such as mindmaps, posters and flashcards, and find past or practice exam papers.

2 Test your knowledge

A large part of your revision is going to be spent here – on *active learning*! Focus your energy on active learning techniques such as flashcard practice, testing your knowledge of the 'cues' section of any Cornell notes, and practising exam questions. Use spaced repetition to structure when and how often you revise each concept.

A secondary element to this activity is to record your weaker areas or the concepts you've been struggling with. You could make a list of the exam questions where you don't feel comfortable about your answers. Separating your flashcards into piles based on your understanding will create this list too.

3 Strengthen weaker areas

You need to also make time to strengthen your weaker areas. Try to identify whether you're struggling because you can't *remember* something or because you don't *understand* it. Then try out the following techniques:

'*I can't remember this.*'

- Add images to your revision material.
- Create a mnemonic to boost your recall.
- Link what you can't remember to material that you can.

'I don't understand this.'

- Find new explanations from books, websites, YouTube, etc.
- Go back to the beginning. Break it down and try to understand the initial material, then look at areas around the concept to try and nab that tricky part.
- Ask for help from your tutor or bring it up in a revision session.
- Discuss the ideas with a friend. Try to explain what you do know and bounce ideas off each other to deepen your understanding.
- Fill the gaps in your knowledge by linking to other concepts or finding case studies and examples.

To structure your revision time, try to spend no more than a quarter of your time creating your revision materials. Then spend the remainder of your time cycling between testing your knowledge and strengthening your weaker areas. As you progress, you should notice your understanding increase and your list of weaker areas decrease.

Create a revision plan

Now you understand how to structure your revision, and the revision techniques that are most effective for *your* exam(s), it's time to create a revision plan. First, make sure you complete the exam investigation exercise, so you know exactly how to fight your exam monster. Next, grab your personal calendar or diary and get comfy for 30 minutes.

Add your key study dates: exam(s); outstanding assignments; classes or revision sessions. Then add in your personal commitments such as events, appointments or work trips, and (hopefully) you should have spaces you can use for your revision. If you don't, then use some of the strategies we looked at earlier in the book such as taking some time off work, rearranging social plans, asking friends and family for help with children, chores or errands, etc.

I recommend trying to schedule in revision sessions, or at least get clear on when you want to try and revise. For example, will you revise on weekdays from 7 am–8 am, Monday to Thursday from 7 pm–9 pm, or all day on Saturdays? Once you know when you want to revise, think about the activities you want to complete and by when:

- When are you going to create your revision materials and when will they be created by?

- When will you start testing your knowledge?
- When will you start revising with practice papers?

Map out a rough plan to focus your revision sessions. You can use this, too, to track your progress and make adjustments if you fall behind. Go back to Chapter 8 on productivity and remind yourself of the best ways to structure your time and study sessions.

How to develop a positive revision mindset

Sometimes it doesn't matter how many tips and tricks we have, if our head's not in the game then we struggle to make progress and see results. Exams are stressful and revising for them can stir up *a lot* of negative thinking – and this can halt your revision in its tracks. Here's some advice for dealing with common revision mindset struggles.

'I'm not an exam person'

Your past exam results do *not* have to dictate your future ones. I've achieved awful exam results in the past; I failed my physics exam and dropped out, and my maths exam grades were so bad my school wanted to kick me out. But once I learned *how* to study and revise effectively, everything changed. I studied a maths module at university and was able to achieve 84 per cent, even though I was achieving grades in the 30–40 per cent range at school.

Being good at exams is a skill that can be learned with dedication and practice. First, understand that exams are not designed to trip you up but instead to test how well you've understood the material. Second, learn some smart revision strategies. You've done this by reading this chapter. Third, believe in yourself and your ability to change. We don't have to stay on the same path in life. We have the ability to stop, rethink and move in a different direction, and that includes stepping onto that high grades highway!

'This is too hard, I want to give up'

Anything worth achieving is difficult. If exams, running marathons and climbing Mount Everest were easy, everyone would do them and they wouldn't be big achievements anymore! It's *completely normal* to get nervous about exam revision… because we *do* get nervous about the things we really care about.

If you get tired, learn to rest, not to quit. If you push yourself too hard for too long, then it's natural you'll want to give up. When you're feeling tired and negative, take a break, get an early night or do something fun so you can come back to your revision fresh and motivated.

Accept that you're going to come across challenges during your revision and they'll be a little easier to deal with. And remember, every time you persevere and overcome something difficult, you'll be stronger for next time and you'll have developed your skills so that the next challenge is easier.

Action steps

- Answer the Exam Investigation questions for each of your exams.
- Understand the best strategies for your specific exam type.
- Create a revision plan for your exam(s) centred around the three core revision activities.
- Create your revision material.
- Get hold of past/practice exam questions and papers.

14
Exam performance

Now you know how to revise effectively, let's focus on the exam itself – how to overcome your fears, what to do in the weeks and days beforehand, and 28 (yes 28!) techniques to use to boost your chances of scoring the high grades you want.

How to develop a positive exam mindset

Here's some advice for overcoming common exam fears.

What if I forget everything?

If you've followed the advice in this book by using active learning techniques and testing your knowledge multiple times – you will remember stuff. Remember, your examiners aren't trying to trip you up and they're also not expecting you to remember every detail to get a good grade.

If you catch yourself panicking before your exam, acknowledge the feeling and then let it drift away. When we do scary things, our brains can try and sabotage us. Instead, focus your energy on what you *can* impact – thinking positively and working hard in your revision.

What if I see a question I don't know how to answer?

Everyone experiences panic at some point during an exam. Your brain is on overdrive and you're hyperaware of your time ticking down. But feeling stressed does not mean you can't do this; it doesn't mean you're not good enough.

If you come to a question you don't understand, stop for a second and take a few slow, deep breaths. Read the question carefully to see if you understand any of the terms. Hopefully some of them will mean something to you and you can start your answer.

If you're still struggling and it's a low-point answer – mark it and come back to it later. If it's a high-mark question – brain dump everything you know about the topic on a piece of scrap paper and see if any relevant points come to you.

How do I stay focused on me?

It can be hard to stay focused during an exam with so many people around you. The person next to you might be scribbling away while you're still thinking. The person in front of you might have already asked for another answer book while you're on the first.

Author and research professor Brené Brown (2014) tweeted, 'Stay in your own lane. Comparison kills creativity & joy.' It's really important to try to focus on you and your own performance; partly because the only thing you have control over is your own effort and work, but also because other students will have different techniques and they may or may not be using their time effectively. So, try not to compare what you *think* they're doing with your own work.

I don't think I've revised enough

On the day of your exam you might not be happy with your revision and feel like you could have done a little more. I don't know anyone who can say they've revised too much, or they wouldn't want more time if it was offered – it's *completely natural* to feel like you could have done more. If you feel unhappy with your revision efforts, you can make improvements for next time.

On the day of your exam, though, you need to *stop* thinking about your revision. You can't alter your past, but you *can* influence your future. It's no use thinking of the revision you didn't do, the sessions you missed or topics you didn't get to cover as many times as you'd liked. What's important is the future: the next few hours until the end of your exam. Walk in there and give it your all. That's the most you can do and, regardless of your results, if you do your best you can walk out of that exam hall with your head held high.

The 4-7-8 exercise

I am a big proponent for the power of breathing. Here's a technique for quelling pre-exam nerves, developed by Dr Andrew Weil (2018). You can do this exercise standing up or sitting down, and you can do it anywhere – in the library, while waiting to go into your exam or in the exam hall while you're waiting for the exam to start.

Breathe in through your nose while counting to four, then hold your breath for a count of seven. Finally, breathe out through your mouth for a count of eight. Repeat this 4-7-8 cycle three more times. Dr Weil explains that you may find it difficult to hold your breath for a count of seven. If so, you can speed up your counting, just make sure you keep the ratio of each part the same: 4-7-8.

Practise this technique during your revision, and then use it before your exam or even during your exam whenever you feel stressed.

How to prepare for your upcoming exam

Here's a list of tasks you want to check off in the days and weeks before each exam.

The few weeks before...

- Check the date, time and location of your exam.
- Plan your journey to and from the exam centre – especially if you haven't been there before.
- Read the exam rules to find out what you can and can't bring into the exam with you.
- Practise writing legibly, fast (for a handwritten exam).

The night before...

- Pack your bag according to the rules for what you need and are allowed.
- Put your revision away after one last session.
- Do something relaxing like having a hot bath, calling a friend or watching your favourite TV show.
- Plan a treat for after your exam the next day.
- Go to bed on time or early and set multiple alarms if you have a morning exam.

The day of...

- Check your bag again for everything you need, including some spare pens.
- Pack water and snacks. Normally, water bottles have to be clear without labels.
- Try and eat something, even if you don't want to. But make sure to stick to what you'd normally eat; the morning of your exam is not the time to try out a new cuisine!
- Check you don't have anything with you that you're not allowed.
- Arrive early so you can get your head in the game.

How to kick butt in your exam

Get ready to discover 28 of my best tips to help you perform at your best, structure your time, and stay calm throughout your exam.

Pre-writing strategies

- *Read the exam instructions* – read the front sheet to check you've been given the right paper. Check what you're allowed on you – if you do have an item you're not allowed then declare it straight away. See if all questions are compulsory – if you do have a choice, check the rules for making your choices.
- *Read, read, underline, read* – to make sure you don't rush into a question and get it wrong, read the question, read it again, underline the key terms, read once more – and then begin.
- *Work out the question timings* – work out the duration of the exam and how many marks are in the paper. Allocate some time at the beginning and end of your exam, then split the rest up to determine how long you have to work on each mark. I'm going to use a three-hour exam worth 80 marks as an example. Let's say you'll need 10 minutes at the start to read the paper and 10 minutes at the end to check and improve your answers. That leaves you with 160 minutes to achieve 80 marks which means you have two minutes to achieve each mark. Remember this number and use it to calculate how long to spend on each question, eg 20 minutes on a 10-mark question.

General writing strategies

- *Mark questions you're unsure about* – if you get stuck on a question, don't waste time. Mark it, move on, and come back to it at the end.
- *Use the number of marks as a clue* – the number of marks per question can give you a clue as to the amount of detail you need to include. For example, for a four-mark question asking you to explain a concept I would recommend you try to write at least four points in your answer. This may vary but it's a useful rule of thumb to remember.
- *Explain what you're doing (if necessary)* – for questions requiring calculations, show your workings to make it clear how you got to your final answer. You may get marks for your workings; you might still get some marks if you get the final answer wrong but your method is correct.
- *Link to module concepts* – an exam is designed to test how much you know about the course, so include module concepts in your answer to achieve marks. This seems straightforward, but I've reviewed a lot of student essays now and I see many students forget to refer back to the theory. Don't be afraid of stating the obvious and showing off what you know.
- *Include examples* – if you are told to use examples and apply theory to a situation or case study in your answer – make sure you do!
- *Include and apply diagrams* – reproduce any relevant module diagrams, charts or graphs if they could enhance your answer. Showing you can draw and label a theoretical diagram is great – even better if you can apply it to a particular situation.

Writing strategies – multiple choice

- *Think of the answer first* – read the question without looking at the options and try to identify the correct answer straight away.
- *If you don't know, guess* – first, check you won't be penalized for guessing wrong answers. Once you know that's not the case, if you don't know an answer, mark it and come back to it. If you run out of time – make an educated guess.
- *Check for errors* – take a few minutes at the end of your exam to double-check your answers – that you haven't left any questions blank or marked too many answers.

Writing strategies – long-answer/essay

- *Always plan your answer* – spend a few minutes at the start of a large question making a quick plan with the key points you want to include. You'll find it easier to stay on track and if your mind goes blank you can check the plan. If you have time at the end of your exam, you can come back and tackle another point from your plan.
- *Check off the plan as you write* – as you're writing your answer, tick off each element of your plan. This will help you keep time, too, as you might realize you need to speed up based on how many points you've covered so far.
- *Aim for coherency* – your marker isn't looking for an unrelated list of points; try and include a one- or two-sentence introduction and then link your main points with signposts and transition words. Finish with a conclusion that wraps up your key findings and links your answer back to the question.
- *Leave space after every answer* – leave half a page to a page in your answer booklet between answers so you have room to add more points later if you have time.
- *Unsure? Brain dump* – if your brain goes blank, take a deep breath and then brain dump everything you know about the topic. As you write down what you *do* know, hopefully some relevant points will jump out that you can use as a springboard into your answer.
- *Switch to bullet points* – if you've run out of time, formal sentences can go out of the window! Switch to bullet points if necessary; you'll likely gain more marks for 10 value-packed bullet points than two well-written points in longer sentences.

Quality control

- *Keep track of the time* – check the time often so you can speed up if necessary.
- *Always move on* – once you know your timings, stick to them religiously. Once your time has run out for a question, finish your sentence, leave some space and move on. You can come back to it during your 'editing' time at the end.

- *Double-check what you're answering* – if you have a choice of questions – double- and triple-check you're answering the right ones!
- *Attempt every question* – if you're running out of time and have two questions left but only really enough time to answer one – try for both. Do the first half of both questions because it's normally easier to gain the first half of a question's marks than the second half.

Finishing strategies

- *Use the time at the end* – use this time to add some more points to your longer answers (in bullet points if necessary), check for errors and cross out any plans that you don't want marking.
- *Never leave early* – exams are designed to take you a certain amount of time. If you finish early, use that time to check your answers and add more value to them.
- *Check all your paperwork* – make sure you've filled out every form and labelled everything correctly.

Wellbeing strategies

- *Sip water throughout* – stay hydrated by taking a few sips of water between answering each question.
- *Take small breaks* – it may feel like you can't stop scribbling but try to stop every few questions for 20 seconds to move your fingers, stretch your wrists and take some deep breaths.
- *Speak up* – if you've forgotten any equipment, tell the invigilator as soon as possible. Similarly, if you feel ill before or during your exam, tell someone. There are often policies in place if you're unwell, but you cannot benefit from these if you don't speak up.

What to do after your exam

When you walk out of that exam hall, you're probably going to feel exhausted, relieved, numb and exhilarated – all at the same time. Make sure you have something fun planned for afterwards because, whatever grade you achieve, and even if you have more exams to revise for… you deserve a reward!

This is easier said than done but try to avoid exam post-mortems. If you start thinking about what you could have or should have written – stop yourself and think about something else.

And, if you're not feeling happy with your performance then I want you to remember this: exams truly aren't everything. You are *not* your exam grade. Whatever grade that piece of paper says – you are an incredible student! You're motivated and hardworking and amazing. Studying is a rollercoaster of a journey and anyone who holds on through the loops and spins deserves to be here.

Action steps

- Practise the 4-7-8 breathing exercise.
- Create a physical checklist of tasks for a few weeks before, the night before, and the day of each exam.
- Note down the in-exam strategies that are relevant to you (out of 28) and embed them into your exam preparation.

Part Six
Personal development

15
Continuous improvement

I've worked with a lot of clients over the last two years to help them change their grades. A student we'll call Kate came to me before the final year of her law degree; her grades were low and it looked like she was going to graduate with third-class honours, which wouldn't be enough to go on to train as a barrister – her dream.

She was starting to believe she was a 'bad' student and thought her dream was impossible to achieve. But, luckily, she decided to try again at aiming for it. Over the course of a few months, we worked on smart essay-writing strategies and improving her study skills. The results for her second-year modules were 53, 54, 62 and 59. After course-correcting, Kate's third-year results were 76, 74 and 76 – which meant she was able to graduate with second-class honours and enrol in her next qualification. Kate thought her dream was impossible, but with a few tweaks and some hard work she was able to turn her dream into a reality!

Some of you may look at your grades and wish they were higher, but you don't know how, or you feel like it's too late. You *can* change the trajectory for your studying success. Your past grades don't have to define your future ones. Maybe you've had a few low marks and you're worried it's too late to change: it almost certainly isn't. As you progress through your studies, your modules will normally become more heavily weighted – which means higher grades in your last modules can often make up for lower grades earlier on.

Throughout your qualification, you'll build more confidence, develop your study skills and become more resilient – all useful tools for pivoting and striking towards a bigger goal if you want it. Remember, there are opportunities to improve your marks and change your direction everywhere – you just need to reach out and take them.

Three ways you can shake up your studying to achieve the grades you really want

1 Try out new study techniques

There are different types of habits. There are those that make your life better, such as brushing your teeth and taking the stairs instead of the lift. Then there are habits that make your life easier, like wearing the same few outfits to work each day, and picking the same gym locker so you don't forget which one you used. Finally, there are the habits that might hinder your life: always reaching for something sweet after dinner (guilty!), scrolling through your phone whenever there's a free moment, and studying in the same way because that's how you've always done it.

It's pretty unlikely that the first study methods you choose for note taking, organizing yourself, essay writing and exam revision are going to be the most effective. What works well for you might not be effective for another student, and the useful methods you've used in one module may not be that valuable for the next.

If you're achieving almost full marks for every essay and exam, then maybe you've found your superstar study strategies. But as you've bought this book, I'm gonna guess you want to achieve higher grades – so try switching up the study methods you use regularly. The end of each module is a great time to reassess which techniques are working for you and which aren't so you can jump into your next round of studying with a refreshed toolkit of study strategies.

Go back through this book often to identify which study strategies you're going to trial. Think about how you learn best, the format of your modules and their importance to your overall grades.

2 Improve with Every. Single. Essay

Your tutors should give you feedback on every essay, explaining why you were allocated your mark and ways to improve next time. If you're not getting much feedback, then please ask for it! You could e-mail your tutor, book a call with them or go to your next office hours session.

Now, no one likes hearing negative feedback. I am pretty good now at seeing all feedback as a chance for improvement, but that doesn't mean critique doesn't feel like a slap in the face sometimes.

When you've worked your butt off on an essay and then receive a low grade, it stings. You might start blaming your tutor, or your university, or yourself. You might rip up or delete the feedback and you might refuse to look at your feedback next time.

All of these things are wasting valuable opportunities to achieve higher grades. A successful student *uses* their feedback to improve their skills. With every essay, they make tweaks and fix errors so their scores climb.

Here's one method for recording your essay feedback and using it to boost your grades. Grab your latest marked essay, your tutor comments, and a piece of blank, lined paper. At the top of the page write the date, your essay title and your mark or grade. Then, split the rest of the page in half with a horizontal line to give you two boxes. Label the top box 'positive points to continue' and the bottom box 'points to improve'.

Scan your feedback for all positive comments about your essay and write them in the top box. These might be, 'clear introduction', 'well-made argument', 'good application of theory', 'great use of the case study', or 'strong conclusion'.

Next, look at your feedback for areas where you lost marks; for example, 'incorrect referencing', 'over the word limit', 'not sure if you understood the question', 'some points lack evidence'. If any points are vague or confusing, then clarify these with your tutor. To note these down, turn the bottom box into two columns with a vertical line. On the left, list those points to improve and then on the right come up with an action you could take to improve that point. For example, if your references are incorrect then your action could be to study your university's style guide to discover the correct way of referencing.

Now it's time to reflect on your own performance: try adding to these lists with your own ideas. First, note down the things you did right in your essay; for example, 'I made a detailed plan before I started writing'. Second, add some of the negative points of your writing process, for example, 'I started my essay too late' or, 'I misunderstood the question so went off on a tangent.' Don't forget to think of action steps to improve each of your negative areas.

File this sheet along with your marked essay and guidance, and use it as a checklist when you're working on your next essay. Make sure every relevant positive point remains and that every negative has been improved or resolved. Do this and your marks will start to climb.

3 Make a habit of reflecting

Sustainable, long-lasting change happens in increments – so get into the habit of tweaking your routines with every study session. Each small change will compound and in a few months your studying will be unrecognizable – in a good way!

At the end of every study session, think about how the session went – how productive you were, and whether you struggled with procrastination, distractions, negative thinking, not knowing what to do or not understanding your material.

Then, set your intention for your next study session by picking one thing you're going to do differently. This could be big or small – here are some ideas:

- Put my phone out of reach.
- Use the Pomodoro Technique.
- Sit at my desk rather than the sofa.
- Pick my priority task before starting.

In our busy student lives, we rarely take time to pause and think about what we've achieved, experienced and learned. We submit one essay and immediately start thinking about the next. We rush, rush, rush, and count down the days until we can complete our course. But stopping to regroup can help you to move further, faster.

I've come up with some questions for you to ask yourself and I want you to promise yourself (and me!) that you'll complete this exercise at least once a year, if not more often. Be sure to dig deep on some of them by asking yourself 'why?' until you get down to the core reason.

So, it's time to get comfy, grab some snacks, and get your self-reflecting on.

Studying self-reflection

Your grades

1 What grades did you achieve in your module(s)?
   - Are you happy with these grades?
   - Why do you think you achieved these grades?

Your study methods

2 What does your note-taking method look like?

   – Has this method worked for you? Could you improve it, or should you try a new method?

3 How do you organize your time and workload? What strategies do you use?

   – Have these methods worked for you? Could you improve them, or should you try new methods?

4 How productive are your study sessions? What techniques do you use to be productive?

   – Have these methods worked for you? Could you improve them, or should you try new methods?

5 What does your essay-writing method look like? How do you plan, write and edit your essay?

   – Have these methods worked for you? Could you improve them, or should you try new methods?

6 What does your exam revision method look like? How do you prepare for your exams?

   – Have these methods worked for you? Could you improve them, or should you try new methods?

Your strengths and achievements

7 What have you achieved this year? Big or small, what have you done that's made you feel proud?

8 Have you accomplished anything you thought was impossible?

9 Which of your personal qualities helped you in your studies?

10 What skills have you learned or developed? What habits have you formed or kicked?

11 What are your studying strengths? What are you good at? *(You're not allowed to leave this blank because EVERYONE has strengths!)*

12 What have you enjoyed learning in your course? What topics have interested you and why?

Your lessons learned

13 What are you disappointed or unhappy about? Do you have any unmet goals?

14 What study skills could you improve?

Your work–life integration

15 Are you happy with how you fit studying into the rest of your life?

16 Are there any problems at work or home that are affecting your studies?
   – If so, is there anything you can do about them?

17 Do you feel supported in your studies by your friends and family around you?
   – If not, is there anything you can do to improve this?

18 How have you coped with your workload? Were you often on track, ahead, or behind?
   – If you regularly fall behind, why is this and what could you do to improve?

Your motivation and mindset

19 What was your most common mental state this year (eg stressed, calm, confident, overwhelmed)?

20 How do you want to feel in your studies moving forward?
   – What could you do to help you achieve this?

21 What are your reasons for studying? Why is your education important to you?

22 How do you celebrate your successes?

You are a good student

Your studying journey will be full of twists and turns. You'll face challenges that may seem impassable at the time, and you'll experience highs and achievements that help you remember why it's all worth it.

A good student isn't someone who never experiences doubt. A good student is someone who develops their study skills so that they can face any challenge their studying throws at them. A good student isn't perfect, but instead they notice when they're going off course and they use their toolkit of study strategies to bring themselves back on track.

By reading this book you have demonstrated that you have the drive, determination and passion to further your education. You now have the study strategies to transform this motivation and hard work into the academic success you want. So, go forth, study like a badass, and make yourself proud.

Action steps

- Complete the feedback exercise for your last essay.
- Reflect on your most recent study session and pick *one* thing you can change to make your next session more effective.
- Complete the studying self-reflection exercise.
- Review how you organize your studies and make tweaks to your methods.
- Review how you take notes and make tweaks to your methods.
- Review how you write essays and make tweaks to your methods.
- Review how you revise for exams and make tweaks to your methods.

REFERENCES

Amabile, T and Kramer, S J (2007) Inner work life: understanding the subtext of business performance, *Harvard Business Review*, May, https://hbr.org/2007/05/inner-work-life-understanding-the-subtext-of-business-performance (archived at https://perma.cc/8XJR-YLE6)

Blackwell, L S, Trzesniewski, K H and Dweck, C S (2007) Implicit theories of intelligence predict achievement across an adolescent transition: a longitudinal study and an intervention, *Child Development*, 78 (1), pp 246–63, https://www.ncbi.nlm.nih.gov/pubmed/17328703 (archived at https://perma.cc/RDQ6-P2R8)

Brown, B (2014) Morning swims are great reminders for the day: Stay in your own lane. Comparison kills creativity & joy, Twitter, 25 June, https://twitter.com/brenebrown/status/481814491730939904?lang=en (archived at https://perma.cc/C7S8-LCCU)

Buzan, T (1974) *Use Your Head*, London, BBC Books

Cirillo, F (2019) Do more and have fun with time management, https://francescocirillo.com/pages/pomodoro-technique (archived at https://perma.cc/33KV-SGKU)

Ducker, C (2017) YOU203 – If it doesn't get scheduled, it doesn't get done, *Youpreneur* [podcast] 20 January, https://www.chrisducker.com/podcast/if-it-doesnt-get-scheduled-it-doesnt-get-done/ (archived at https://perma.cc/PV8U-KA2E)

Duckworth, A L and Seligman, M E P (2005) Self-discipline outdoes IQ in predicting academic performance of adolescents, *Psychological Science*, 16 (12), pp 939–44, https://journals.sagepub.com/doi/abs/10.1111/j.1467-9280.2005.01641.x (archived at https://perma.cc/B5JW-TLFF)

Dweck, C S (2017) *Mindset: Changing the way you think to fulfil your potential*, London, Robinson

Encyclopaedia Britannica (2018) *Hermann Ebbinghaus: German psychologist*, https://www.britannica.com/biography/Hermann-Ebbinghaus (archived at https://perma.cc/HB8Q-K5CS)

Ferriss, T (2016) The one-handed concert pianist, Nicholas McCarthy, *The Tim Ferriss Show* [podcast] 19 July, https://tim.blog/2016/07/19/the-one-handed-concert-pianist-nicholas-mccarthy/ (archived at https://perma.cc/86X7-88P9)

Freudenberger, H J (1974) Staff burnout, *Journal of Social Issues*, 30, pp 159–65, https://spssi.onlinelibrary.wiley.com/doi/abs/10.1111/j.1540-4560.1974.tb00706.x (archived at https://perma.cc/4ZTY-L2W5)

Froome, C (2014) *The Climb: The Autobiography*, London, Penguin

Gollwitzer, P M (1993) Goal achievement: the role of intentions, *European Review of Social Psychology*, 4 (1), pp 141–85, https://www.researchgate.net/publication/233894856_Goal_Achievement_The_Role_of_Intentions (archived at https://perma.cc/76RZ-WQ4D)

References

Gollwitzer, P M (1999) Implementation intentions: strong effects of simple plans, *American Psychologist*, **54** (7), pp 493–503, http://www.psych.nyu.edu/gollwitzer/99Goll_ImpInt.pdf (archived at https://perma.cc/XU3M-3N2U)

Hanson, R (2010) Take in the good, https://www.rickhanson.net/take-in-the-good/ (archived at https://perma.cc/22NP-AESA)

HESA (2018) HE student enrolments by personal characteristics, https://www.hesa.ac.uk/data-and-analysis/students/whos-in-he (archived at https://perma.cc/8Y8W-LDKB)

King, S (1981) *Danse Macabre*, New York, Everest House

Lleras, A and Ariga, A (2011) Brief and rare mental 'breaks' keep you focused: deactivation and reactivation of task goals pre-empt vigilance decrements, *Cognition*, **118** (3), pp 439–43, https://www.sciencedirect.com/science/article/pii/S0010027710002994?via%3Dihub (archived at https://perma.cc/9EQK-GXT6)

Medina, J (2008) *Brain Rules: 12 principles for surviving and thriving at work, home and school*, Seattle, Pear Press

Meyer, D E and Kieras, D E (1997) A computational theory of executive cognitive processes and multiple-task performance: Part 1. basic mechanisms, *Psychological Review*, **104** (1), pp 3–65, https://www.ncbi.nlm.nih.gov/pubmed/9009880 (archived at https://perma.cc/8SC6-KN7U)

Mitra, S (2007) Sugata Mitra: Kids can teach themselves, *TED*, https://www.ted.com/talks/sugata_mitra_shows_how_kids_teach_themselves (archived at https://perma.cc/U5FN-S3J4)

Mueller, P A and Oppenheimer, D M (2014) The pen is mightier than the keyboard: advantages of longhand over laptop note taking, *Psychological Science*, **25** (6), pp 1159–68, https://journals.sagepub.com/doi/abs/10.1177/0956797614524581 (archived at https://perma.cc/5YVP-9FQR)

Newsweek (2015) Michael Jordan didn't make varsity – at first, https://www.newsweek.com/missing-cut-382954 (archived at https://perma.cc/2RHA-BTTM)

Oppenheimer, D M (2006) Consequences of erudite vernacular utilized irrespective of necessity: problems with using long words needlessly, *Applied Cognitive Psychology*, **20** (2), pp 139–56, https://onlinelibrary.wiley.com/doi/abs/10.1002/acp.1178 (archived at https://perma.cc/RDH5-7CM9)

Oswald, A (2016) J K Rowling shares photos of her rejection letters for 'inspiration', *Business Insider*, https://www.businessinsider.com/jk-rowling-rejection-letters-2016-3?r=UK (archived at https://perma.cc/C5NK-FFAM)

Pauk, W and Owens, R J Q (2013) *How to Study in College*, Boston, Cengage Learning

Pooh's Grand Adventure: The Search for Christopher Robin (1997) Directed by Karl Geurs [Film] California, Walt Disney Home Video

Pressfield, S (2011) *Do the Work: Overcome resistance and get out of your own way*, Black Irish Entertainment LLC

Robbins, M (2017) *The 5 Second Rule: The surprisingly simple way to live, love, and speak with courage*, Nashville, Post Hill Press

Rowling, J K (1999) *Harry Potter and the Prisoner of Azkaban*, London, Bloomsbury

Rowling, J K (2016) I wasn't going to give up until every single publisher turned me down, but I often feared that would happen, *Twitter*, 25 March, https://twitter.com/jk_rowling/status/713292055284424704?lang=en (archived at https://perma.cc/8LDY-Y2WJ)

Sharma, R (2014) Don't confuse activity with productivity. Many people are simply busy being busy, Twitter, 25 May, https://twitter.com/robinsharma/status/470746180301762561 (archived at https://perma.cc/65BU-FJ32)

Shih, Y N, Huang, R H and Chiang, H Y (2012) Background music: effects on attention performance, *Work*, 42 (4), pp 573–78, https://www.ncbi.nlm.nih.gov/pubmed/22523045 (archived at https://perma.cc/9APS-7JUG)

Solan, M (2016) Back to school: learning a new skill can slow cognitive aging, *Harvard Health*, https://www.health.harvard.edu/blog/learning-new-skill-can-slow-cognitive-aging-201604279502 (archived at https://perma.cc/S2KE-46AT)

SuperMemo (2019) *SuperMemo*, https://www.supermemo.com/en (archived at https://perma.cc/8RB5-T6F5)

Taylor, W L (1953) 'Cloze procedure': a new tool for measuring readability, *Journalism & Mass Communication Quarterly*, 30 (4), pp 415–33, https://journals.sagepub.com/doi/abs/10.1177/107769905303000401 (archived at https://perma.cc/2PT3-CU88)

Tracy, B (2001) *Eat That Frog! 21 great ways to stop procrastinating and get more done in less time*, Oakland, Berrett-Koehler

Trapani, G (2007) Jerry Seinfeld's productivity secret, *Lifehacker*, https://lifehacker.com/281626/jerry-seinfelds-productivity-secret (archived at https://perma.cc/7R8S-HHWJ)

Trei, L (2007) New study yields instructive results on how mindset affects learning, *Stanford*, https://news.stanford.edu/news/2007/february7/dweck-020707.html (archived at https://perma.cc/B54U-3988)

Turner, J (2015) *The Fringe Hours*, Grand Rapids, MI, Revell

Vossel, S, Geng, J J and Fink, G R (2013) Dorsal and ventral attention systems: distinct neural circuits but collaborative roles, *The Neuroscientist*, 20 (2), pp 150–59, https://journals.sagepub.com/doi/full/10.1177/1073858413494269 (archived at https://perma.cc/3XKP-FW8E)

Weil, A (2018) Three breathing exercises and techniques, https://www.drweil.com/health-wellness/body-mind-spirit/stress-anxiety/breathing-three-exercises/ (archived at https://perma.cc/9AHF-PCJH)

Winch, G (2014) *Emotional First Aid: Healing rejection, guilt, failure, and other everyday hurts*, New York, Plume Books

Wohl, M J A, Pychyl, T A and Bennett, S H (2010) I forgive myself, now I can study: how self-forgiveness for procrastinating can reduce further procrastination, *Personality and Individual Differences*, **48** (7), pp 803–08, https://www.sciencedirect.com/science/article/pii/S0191886910000474?via%3Dihub (archived at https://perma.cc/9UAP-8F8R)

Woźniak, P (2018) The true history of spaced repetition, *SuperMemo*, https://www.supermemo.com/en/articles/history (archived at https://perma.cc/UN6G-4G74)

Wozniak, R H (1999) *Classics in Psychology, 1855–1914: Historical essays*, Bristol, Thoemmes Press

INDEX

Note: page numbers in *italic* indicate figures or tables

4-7-8 technique 196–97
5Ds 122–23
5 second rule 121

academic writing skills 163–64
active learning 180–81, 191, 195
    flashcards 182–85, 191
    practice exam papers 186–87
    quizzes 185–86
A-levels, value of 1
Amabile, T and Kramer, S 70

backups, making 82–84, 154
    digital materials 83
    hard copies 84
'best study self', finding your 96–97, *97*
Blackwell, L et al 51
Brain Rules 183
    essay writing 169
    in exams 201
    Pomodoro Technique 99, 102–04, 118, 208
        extending your breaks 124
    study breaks 31–32, 101–02
        avoiding burnout 128–29
Brown, Brené 196
burnout 125, 127–29
Buzan, Tony 147

CamScanner 14, 84
change, resistance to 117
childcare, juggling 38, 122
Cirillo, France 102
classes 133–39
    after class 137
    attending, importance of 134
    focus, maintaining 137, 139
    lectures 133
    note-taking 136–37, 143
    office hours 133
    practicals 134
    preparing for 135–36
    tutorials 133
Climb, The 57
closed book exams 178, 188
cloze tests 184

Cold Turkey 85
commitments, working around 98
commute, using your 107–08
constructive criticism 55, 62
continuous improvement 205–11
    feedback, getting 206–07
    reflecting 208–10
    study methods, changing 206
Cornell method 148–50, *149*
critical thinking 166–68
    analysis 167
    application 167–68
    evaluation 168

Danse Macabre 53
deadline pressure 114
discipline 11–12, 53, 95
distance learning 17–21
    advantages 17–19
    disadvantages 19–21
distractions, avoiding 36, 40, 85
    multitasking 104–05, 118
    procrastination 115, 118
Do the Work 168
DropBox 83, 154
Ducker, Chris 23, 99
Duckworth, A and Seligman, M 53
Dweck, Carol 51

'eat the frog' method 71–72, 119
Ebbinghaus, Hermann 181
Economist, The 31
essay-based exams 177, 187–88, 200
essays, writing 155–71
    editing stage 168–71
        breaks, taking 169
        editing checklist 170–71
    planning stage 155–60
        essay document, your 156–57
        question, understanding the 157–59, *158–59*
        sources, finding 160
    writing stage 160–68
        academic writing skills 163–64
        conclusion 165–66
        critical thinking 166–68

Index

essays, writing (*continued*)
    evidence, giving 160, 163
    first draft 161
    introduction 164–65
    objective, being 164
    points, identifying your 161
    signposts 161–62
    transitions 162
evidence, giving 160, 163
exams, revising for 175–94
    active learning 180–81, 191, 195
        flashcards 182–85, 191
        practice exam papers 186–87
        quizzes 185–86
    closed book exams 178, 188
    cloze tests 184
    essay-based exams 177, 187–88, 200
    exam concept mind maps 179
    exam details 175–76
    mindset 193–94
    mnemonic devices 184
    multiple choice exams 176–77, 187, 199
    multiple exams, juggling 189–90
    open book exams 179, 189
    passive learning 180
    revision material 191
    revision planning 192–93
    seen exams 178, 188
    short-answer exams 177, 187
    spaced repetition 181–82, *182*, 185, 191
        forgetting curve, the 181
    unseen exams 177–78, 188
    weaker areas, strengthening 191–92
exams, taking 195–02
    breaks, taking 201
    hydration 201
    mindset
        4-7-8 technique 196–97
        focus, maintaining 196
        panic, mastering 195
    preparation 197–98
    pre-writing strategies 198
    rewards 202
    writing strategies 199–01
        essay-based exams 200
        finishing 201
        multiple choice exams 199
        quality control 200–01
extensions, asking for 123, 125

family, balancing study with 38, 108–11
    boundaries, setting 108–09
    childcare, juggling 38, 122
    expectation setting 109
    family study time 110
    support, getting 110–11

fear of failure 54, 61, 115, 119–20
feedback, getting 206–07
Ferriss, Tim 57
filing 32, 34
    digital materials 80–82, *81*, 153
    hard copies 79–80
flashcards 182–85, 191
flexible, being 35
    and goal setting 46
    and motivation 91
focus, maintaining
    in class 137, 139
    in exams 196
forgetting curve, the 181
Freudenberger, Herbert 127
'fringe hours' 106
Froome, Chris 57

goals, setting 39–47
    actions, identifying 43
    brainstorming 41
    flexibility 46
    grade-based 40
    habit-based 40, 41
    and motivation 40, 42–43, 91
    number to set 45
    obstacles 44
    'quick wins' 42
    reviewing 46–47
    rewards 44
    sub-goals 42
    support, getting 44
    tracking progress 45–46
Gollwitzer, Peter 92
Google 11
    Google Drive 83, 154
gratitude, practicing 65
growth mindset 10

Hanson, Rick 62
'happy things jar' 73–74
Harry Potter 54
    Harry Potter and the Prisoner of Azkaban 65
HESA 14
hydration 99, 201

imposter syndrome 59
Inc. 31
independent learning skills 9–12
    discipline 11–12, 53, 95
    initiative 10–11
    motivation 9–10, 67–76
    organizational skills 10, 28–29, 34, 79–94
    problem-solving skills 10–11

self-belief 9–10
self-development focus 11
time management 10, 28–29
initiative 10–11
inner critic, your 62–63
inspiration, finding 56–57
IQ, importance of 53

Jordan, Michael 53–54

Kids Can Teach Themselves 57
King, Stephen 53

lectures 133
Lleras, A and Ariga, A 101–02

mature student, being a 14–17
advantages 14–15
disadvantages 15–17
McCarthy, Nicholas 57
Medina, John 183
Meyer, D and Kieras, D 105
Microsoft
Excel 89
OneDrive 83, 154
Word 90, 171
mind maps *147*, 147–48
exam concept mind maps 179
MindMeister 148
mindset 51–66
constructive criticism 55, 62
4-7-8 technique 196–97
exam performance 195–97
focus, maintaining 196
panic, mastering 195
exam revision 193–94
fixed mindset 51, 54–55, 56
fear of failure 54, 61
gratitude, practicing 65
growth mindset 10, 51, 53, 54
imposter syndrome 59
inner critic, your 62–63
inspiration, finding 56–57
joy, finding the 66
mistakes, importance of 55–56, 63
motivation 58
negativity bias 62
perseverance 56
procrastination 58
reframing 60, 64, *64*, 120
self-sabotage 58
talent, importance of 52–54
tracking progress 63
mistakes, importance of 55–56, 63
Mitra, Sugata 57

mnemonic devices 184
motivation 9–10, 67–76
accountability 91
breaking out of a rut 71, 118
'eat the frog' method 71–72, 119
ebbs and flows 35
everyday motivation 68, 69, 90
and flexibility 91
and goal setting 40, 42–43, 91
'happy things jar' 73–74
and mindset 58, 70–71
and momentum 70, 76
motivational quotes 72
'no excuse' tasks 75–76, 118
'one day' motivation 67–68, *68*, 90
procrastination 71
Progress Principle 70
'quick wins' 71, 120
rewards 72–73, 119
and self-care 127
sub-tasks, creating 72
support, getting 37
tracking progress 73, 119
Mueller, P and Oppenheimer, D 152
multiple choice exams 176–77, 187, 199

negativity bias 62
Newsweek 53
'no excuse' tasks 75–76, 118
note-taking 136–37, 140–54
copying notes 140–41
Cornell method 148–50, *149*
during class 136–37, 143
highlighting 141
identifying what's important 144–45
matching notes to assignment
  types 142–43
mind maps *147*, 147–48
Outlining method *151*, 151–52
process of 146–47
typing 153
verbatim notes 141, 143
writing by hand 152–53

objective, being 164
obstacles
and goal setting 44
planning for 92
office hours 133
open book exams 179, 189
Open University 18, 89
organizational skills 10, 28–29, 34, 79–94
backups 82–84, 154
digital materials 83
hard copies 84

organizational skills (*continued*)
    filing 32, 34
        digital materials 80–82, *81*, 153
        hard copies 79–80
    procrastination 115
    study plan, your 88–90, *90*
        due dates, tracking 10, 33, 88–89
    study space, your 29–30, 35–36, 84–88
        distractions, avoiding 85
        music, choosing 86–87, 96, 129
    work-life balance 92–94
organizational skills 10
Oswald, A 54
Outlining method *151*, 151–52
overwhelm 115, 121–23
    5Ds 122–23
    brain download 121–22

panic, mastering 195
passive learning 180
Pauk, W and Owens, R 148
paying for your studies 15
perfection, the pursuit of 35, 60
perseverance 56
Pomodoro Technique 99, 102–04, 118, 208
    breaks, extending your 124
    multitasking 105
    rules of 103–04
    when you've fallen behind 126
Pooh's Grand Adventure 34
power naps 124
practicals 134
practice exam papers 186–87
Pressfield, Steven 168
problem-solving skills 10–11
procrastination 58, 71, 113–21
    5 second rule 121
    anti-procrastination strategies 118–20
    deadline pressure 114
    fear of failure 54, 61, 115, 119–20
    guilt 113
    procrastination lists 103
    reasons for 113, 114–15
    resistance to change 117
productivity 41, 95–112
    'best study self', finding your 96–97, *97*
    commitments, identifying 98
    and multitasking 104–05
    planner template 99–101, *100*
    Pomodoro Technique 102–04, 118
        multitasking 105
        rules of 103–04
    priorities, identifying 98
    self-discipline 11–12, 53, 95
    study breaks 31–32, 101–02

study sessions, scheduling 99
    vs being busy 95
    as a workplace learner
        'fringe hours' 106
        key tasks 106–07
        studying on your commute 107–08
Progress Principle 70

'quick wins' 71
    study goals 42, 120
quizzes 185–86

reframing 60, 64, *64*, 120
rewards 72–73
    after achieving a study goal 44, 119
    after an exam 202
Robbins, Mel 120–21
Rowling, J K 54, 65

Scannable 84, 154
seen exams 178, 188
Seinfeld, Jerry 45–46
self-belief 9–10
self-care 127
self-discipline 11–12, 53, 95
self-sabotage 58
seminars 133
Sharma, Robin 95
Shih, Y et al 86
short-answer exams 177, 187
Simple Mind+ 148
Solan, M 17
sources, finding 160
spaced repetition 181–82, *182*, 185, 191
    forgetting curve, the 181
stationery and office supplies 27–28
study plan, your 88–90, *90*
    due dates, tracking 10, 33, 88–89
study space, your 29–30, 35–36, 84–88
    distractions, avoiding 85
    music, choosing 86–87, 96, 129
Sunday Study Review 111
support network, your 36–38, 126
    and goal setting 44

talent, importance of 52–54
Taylor, Wilson 184
TED talks 57
time management 10, 28–29
tiredness, coping with *132*, 123–25
    burnout 125
    exam revision 194
    power naps 124
Tracy, Brian 71–72
Trapani, G 46

Trei, L 52
Turner, Jessica 106
tutor relationship, your 33
   distance learning 20–21
   essay planning 160
   essay/exam support 138
   feedback, taking 206–07
   and goal setting 44
   office hours 133
   support, getting 125
   thanking your tutor 137
tutorials 133

Über das Gedchtnis 181
unseen exams 177–78, 188

Vossel, S et al 86

Weil, Andrew 196
Winch, Guy 104
Wohl, M et al 119–20
Work 86
work-life balance 92–94
workplace learning 21–26, 105–08
   advantages 21–22
   disadvantages 22–26
   'fringe hours' 106
   studying on your commute 107–08
workshops 133
Woźniak, Piotr 181, 183

YouTube 11, 66